In an ideal world, a man would profit from another's wisdom so he could be successful in relationships from a young age, but in modern society he's misinformed and therefore his relationships are sabotaged before they even start. Here, Franco, Joseph and David provide a guide to having successful relationships with real advice that works in the real world.
— Paradise, author of *21st Century Fox*

For personal coaching and more great work from the Author:

Joseph W. South
amazon.com/author/josephwsouth

joseph.went.south@gmail.com

Practical Female Psychology

for the Practical Man

♣ Joseph ◊ David ♡ Franco ♠

Revision 642. Originally published on June 18, 2008 by Joseph W. South, David Clare and Franco. This version was published on September 1, 2019 by Joseph W. South.

DISCLAIMER: The material in this book is provided for entertainment purposes only. Use of this material by the reader is done solely at his or her own discretion and risk. The authors and editors do not accept any legal responsibility for such use.
The reader understands and agrees that the information contained herein does not constitute medical advice. The material within is not a substitute for psychiatric treatment, psychological counselling, or any other type medical or professional treatment. The reader hereby agrees to hold harmless the authors, editors and publishers of this book from any liability or harm arising out of reading this book or any attempt to apply the knowledge contained herein.
All readers are responsible for any use or misuse of the material presented in this work.
NO WARRANTY EXPRESS OR IMPLIED IS MADE FROM THIS WORK.
Illustrations: Free Documentation licensed illustrations from Wikipedia are used in this book. SCN: Spartan Thunder

The authors dedicate the work to the man serious about women, who is willing to examine his own life to determine "Is what I have what I really want?" And who is ready and willing to take action, immediately.

The authors also dedicate this work to the women in their lives, past present and future. Those mothers, sisters, friends and girlfriends, dates, lovers, flings, partners, wives and all those women who have been our inspiration, our muses throughout our lives. We hope that the man or men in your lives are, or will learn to be, your every thought of a man.

Joseph W. South: In particular, I dedicate this book to Olivia, who in three wonderful years has taught me a great deal about patience, empathy, and sensitivity to the feminine spirit.

Acknowledgments

We especially thank all the men we have met who have become determined to "get this part of my life handled" and who have graciously and freely shared an enormous amount of experience with the authors.

We are deeply grateful to numerous academic scholars as well as several members of the seduction community; people who have dedicated their lives to the understanding of the female mind and body and to sharing their wisdom with their fellow man.

Contents

About the Authors

David Clare

I am in my mid-40s. I was married for eight years, in what is now referred to as a co-dependent relationship, to a woman I deeply loved. My exasperation and frustration with her behavior resulted in my losing attraction for her. I was unable to lead her effectively, but my strength of commitment to the sanctity of our marriage transcended what I considered to be relatively trivial concerns of sexual and emotional fulfillment. She left. I still believe, in the long-term scheme of things, considering the capriciousness that life deals us even in the best case, that the security, financial stability and deep caring that I gave her would have been to her best benefit. Had she stayed, I still believe we would have been able to work it out.

Now that I understand a lot more about how women work, I won't ever be in such a situation again. I now have the tools to emotionally and sexually satisfy women. More importantly, I have the skills to ensure I choose women that sexually and emotionally satisfy *me*. I feel as if I am in paradise, living in a large urban area with large numbers of attractive, successful women, and so few men with the skill to excite their imaginations!

Furthermore, I now have skills for managing different kinds of relationships. Not all women are high-speed-rail bound for matrimony at all costs, a tremendously self-limiting belief ingrained in the so-called "men's movement." Women are infinitely more complex than that, and always have been, as authors such as Casanova delighted in telling us hundreds of years ago. That I choose to be in one form of relationship over another is *my* choice.

Part of the motivation for pouring my energy into this book comes from disillusionment with the standard self-help material available on bookshelves everywhere. I could not find anything at all that offered a view of masculinity, which didn't involve me ultimately submitting to a point of view that felt emasculating and deeply unnatural. Applying the information in those books did not help me save my marriage, and more importantly, it didn't help me to be a better person.

I felt I had nowhere to turn, that is, until I found a group of men on the internet, united by a common delight in women. My experience was not unique! Other men were dealing with the exact same issues I was dealing with. Other men felt what I felt. Other men were tired of being a sympathetic, generous man being automatically spurned even by unattractive women! Can you feel me here? Ridiculous isn't it?

Most importantly, I learned through applying "seduction techniques" that everything to do with "picking up chicks" applies just as well, *if not more so*, to women in relationships. Picking up different women requires learning a few basic skills which can be applied repetitively: same schtick, different chick. In a relationship, you are picking up the same woman, over and over and over again. Now that, friend, requires some A++, rock-solid, locked-on, hard core skills.

And that's what we're all about.

Joseph W. South

I am in my late 30's. I am a single white male, divorced. According to all the self-help books on dating and relationships, I have a lot going for me: good fashion sense, decent looks and financial independence. I am unusually kind, loving and caring. However, as I learned from reading such books as *No More Mr. Nice Guy* by Dr. Robert Glover, my abundant "niceness" was mostly just a facade covering over the real personality of a fairly aggravated man.

Until recently, women were a complete mystery to me. What's worse, I *believed* that I actually understood women, despite experiencing a lot of frustration and lonely nights. I had no problem finding a girlfriend, which was probably due in part to some of my qualities that I've listed above. But having lasting, happy relationships, and having a woman truly adore me for who I am in a lasting way is another matter.

Five years after first stumbling across a David DeAngelo product on the internet, I now date several women both in my hometown and abroad. Every one of these relationships are superior to any I had before, even to those prior occasions when I felt like I had found "the one."

I now realize I can generate attraction and have a relationship with a wide variety of women; however, my standards have risen and I am much more selective about who I will get intimate with. Ironically, as my standards have risen, so too have my options. Beautiful women no longer intimidate me and I see that physical beauty is, in fact, very common. Now, I can focus on getting the type of relationship that I want, and I am not merely idolizing women's bodies like I used to.

I have devoted my life to reading, studying, meeting people and entrepreneurial ventures. My father was a successful, self-made businessman who was plagued with confusion about women and their nature right until his death. He would often complain to me and my siblings about ill treatment from his wife, and I could never understand why my father would remain with a woman whom he obviously did not like. I silently vowed to myself to resolve once and for all the questions of relationships, sexual attraction, and achieving respect from the women I encounter in my life. I deeply believe that these are things that every man wants, and I have the passion and determination to find that for myself and to help other men to do the same.

I now enjoy happy, sexual and platonic relationships with several women, with each woman's knowledge and consent.

Franco

I am a man in his middle 40s and what many might consider to be a "bad guy." I am a businessman and also a medical professional in a field where I am in daily contact with the darkest and most tragic aspects of human nature.

I have been since childhood what you would call a "Natural," as in a natural playboy: a man who likes to have sex and relationships with a lot of women, knows how to achieve that and feels no guilt feeling about it because it is for him completely natural. A Natural is a guy who belongs to a mostly-misunderstood sexual minority, just like gays or lesbians. A Natural is a guy who was never under the influence of the Madonna/whore complex and who has been loving multiple women since he was young.

Usually, a Natural is not aware of being such, and that was my Karma until 1995 when, at the end of my former marriage, I slowly became conscious, in a rather tragic way, of the shocking fact that, given certain circumstances, I could be emotionally dangerous to women in this society.

I realized at a certain point that I was emotionally dangerous to women because as a "Natural" I was not able nor I was motivated in the slightest way to repress my male sexual instinct, as many men do. I have found in my life that a man like me can be highly arousing to women, and at the same time put them in emotional danger.

Many men make an agreement to giving up their own masculinity and sexuality in exchange for sex and affection. These men accept being emasculated by a woman whom they feel has taken the role of the Madonna in their life. I never did that; I just continuously went for what I wanted. In my life there were no "Madonnas" and there were no "whores," only women. I was unable to consider all women to be whores as many other men do. I simply loved all the women I had dealings with, and I am proud of it.

As a Natural I was not completely conscious of the fact that loving women for exactly who they are can even be emotionally dangerous in our society. When I realized that loving women in this way can in fact be emotionally dangerous, I decided that I would start to help other men to love women for who they are, *without* putting the women in emotional danger.

Too many men do not see women for who they are. So many men could make a better life for themselves if they would come to understand the real nature of the female psyche, learn how to love women for who they are, and even help to make women into better people. I have been in a wonderful position to get a deep understanding of these things, because throughout my life I have loved with all my heart and dedication women, especially those women your mother and father warned you about.

More information

The authors provide a wealth of resources in order to help you to apply this material and continuously enhance the richness of your relationships with women, including one-on-one coaching, audio programs, and other articles and books designed to help with specific aspects of male-female relationships. You may find out more about the authors and the products and services that they offer by

You may find out more about the authors and the products and services that they offer by emailing joseph.went.south@gmail.com

Introduction

The first rule of Fight Club: You do not talk about Fight Club. — Tyler Durden, from the movie "Fight Club"

OUR book isn't for everyone. Some men are deeply angry, bitter or cynical about women in general; we can't help you. You must first let those destructive emotions dissipate. Such emotions are frightening to women, such that they actually produce a physical, instinctual response within her. Even a physically small man becomes a big, scary guy throwing a big, scary fit when he allows his angry emotions to run amok. Women have a biologically hardwired panic reaction to such behavior, and they will avoid men exhibiting signs of it.

Men who are happy in their marriages have little need for our material, although we guarantee they will read it and find themselves saying, "Hey, that's what I do too!" And we believe that even happy men will find nuggets of wisdom that allow them to be more than just happy. We're talking real wisdom, that will allow men to absolutely delight the women in their lives and teach men to take their relationships to the next level.

This book *is* for men who love women and want to improve their relationships with them and achieve maximum well-being for both parties.

The Modern, Western Woman

Men and women in our modern society have become emotionally and psychologically distant from each other. In some countries — such as the United States and western Europe — the situation has worsened. Women today have far greater civil rights than men, yet continue to engage in political battles against men whom they view as their common oppressor. This process creates resentment in men, who feel that they are no longer being appreciated as fathers and husbands. Many men react to this by engaging in infidelity with other women (or even men!) and/or withdrawing from their responsibilities as fathers and husbands.

The modern, western woman is free to explore as wide of a range of sexual experience as she desires, with very little risk to her physical health and safety. However, women are still subject to the dictates of biology, which have evolved over millions of years, and women still suffer from culturally-induced biases that hinder them from truly enjoying their sexuality. In this book, we will demonstrate vividly the ramifications of both biology and culture on the modern woman, and we will show you how to help her to overcome these biases, for the rich enjoyment of both of you.

This Book is for You

If women seem mysterious to you, it simply indicates *your* lack of experience or knowledge, nothing more. It's nothing to be ashamed of, but it *is* something to rectify.

For men who find women a complete mystery, there is hope: much of female behavior can be predicted, as Franco is famous for saying, "with mathematical precision!" Think about it. The average college woman has dated many men, perhaps 6 or 12, or possibly (almost certainly) many more. She has a wealth of resources at her disposal for dealing with men, ranging from gossip with friends and coworkers, to shelves of books in the bookstore, to any of dozens of magazines such as *Cosmopolitan*; all of these dedicated to the art of maintaining attraction and connection with men. What do men enjoy that's comparable? Nothing! And in the realm of divorce, custody and domestic violence law, today's woman almost always enjoys far more rights than any man does.

The majority of men today do not possess very many tools that work effectively when it comes to understanding and dealing with the opposite sex. Go ahead and take a visit to your local bookstore. Browse the books on relationships, and the books authored by women purporting to tell you "what women want" and "how to treat women." Does this stuff actually work? Well, with divorce rates at an all-time high, with divisions between the sexes even more pronounced than ever, we would have to say "no, it does not work!". *In our own personal experience, the prevailing, mainstream dating and relationship advice does not work!* However, once you unravel the mysteries of *subcommunication* with our help, you will read these books in a whole different light. Very much like reading between the lines, you will begin to see that what women say isn't exactly what they mean, at least not in terms of male language. You must pay attention to *how* women say what they say — and equally importantly — to what they have left *unsaid*. As we will show, these same books can actually become a gold mine of information once a man understands how to use these resources properly.

When relationships are handled properly, modern, western women provide men with unparalleled opportunity for personal growth and enrichment. Women today have more money, more power, and more education than at any time in history. Many women today can completely financially support a man and a family. Women can train their minds and develop their bodies to help even the score *physically* with men, and therefore can be in less danger from physical assault than ever before in history.

The basis of our book is the celebration of femininity and female sexuality. We absolutely adore women! All three of us, in our everyday lives, are passionate lovers of women, both inside and outside the bedroom. However, we do not worship women. We simply treat them as truly equal partners, and insist that they act as responsible adults in their interactions with us. We — along with the women with us — get what we need and want out of our relationships. As importantly, we have learned to choose women receptive to what we are able to bring to relationships. With most women, we step up to the leadership position that we naturally possess as men — which most women absolutely crave, whether they admit to that or not.

Setting the Stage

Have you ever met a man who says of his wife, "She's the boss!"? No doubt you have, and no doubt you've noticed that when a man says something like this, he *means* it, as if his wife figuratively carries his balls in her purse. Do you find this sort of thing to be vaguely (or extremely) alarming? We certainly do, for many, many reasons.

Fundamentally, we find this type of situation alarming because, in our actual, real world experience with women, such men are invariably less than delighted with their marriages. At the same time these men feel powerless. They also suspect, often quite correctly, that their wives don't really respect them. Ask any one of these men, "Hey, how's sex with the wife?" and most likely you will get answers ranging from "Sex? What's that?" to a hostile *"That's none of your fucking business."* In our experience, we rarely meet the man who smiles, saying "She treats me well."

You've probably experienced a similar pattern when it comes single men. Of course, there *are* single men that have happy and vibrant sex lives. But teenage boys and young men are often taught through locker room antics that it's ok and even a lot of fun to brag about sexual conquests that are exaggerated, and that many times, never even happened. And then there are other men who begin a relationship and enjoy incredible sex at the beginning, only to find that over time, the sex diminishes as the woman's emotional demands increase. You may have even experienced the pain that comes when you love your girlfriend so much and would do anything to please her, and yet the harder you try, the more distant she gets. This can be extremely frustrating for a man.

We are here to tell you: It doesn't have to be this way!

We will show you throughout the pages of this book how you can escape all manner of emotional traps and manipulation. We will teach you ways of changing *yourself,* thus allowing you to lead yourself into a happy future with an adoring woman. We give you practical advice every step of the way, with real examples drawn from our personal experiences.

Our Motivation

So, why did we decide to write this book about women, anyway? We want to help our fellow men to understand, appreciate and love women for who and what they are. We want to destroy a myth: the myth that women cannot be understood. Women *can* be understood, as Franco likes to say "with mathematical precision," and women can be loved for who they are, with the greatest love. We want to share with *you* what we have found actually works with happy women in our lives, women who do indeed treat us well.

When the three of us met each other for the first time and became friends, one thing was clear from the start: all of us love women for the wonderful human beings that they are. Each of us consider it most important to *unconditionally love women for who women are, rather than who we would naively wish them to be.*

How to Read this Book

Throughout this book, we repeatedly share our beliefs about women and female behavior. We are much less concerned with proving any irrefutable truth than we are with the efficacy of our beliefs. The framework we present is based on biological and evolutionary principles, but we don't insist on causality. These principles simply provide a coherent structure upon which to hang our experience with women, and our observations of women's behavior.

Each chapter describes a key component in the panorama of practical female psychology, yet each chapter is inter-related. To get the most out of this book, you may find the need to read it more than once. We use many broad generalizations to isolate and precisely describe various facets of female behavior.

The reader must understand that applying any broad generalization to a specific woman requires calibrating the principle to the women at hand. No one woman embodies a stereotype, yet all women share common traits in greater or lesser degree.

We wish all of you a wonderful journey during your reading of this book. We sincerely hope that this book will be of help to many, many men the world over, as they strive for their lifelong, natural desire to make the women that they love exceedingly happy.

1 The Role of Evolution

Whatever is done from love always occurs beyond good and evil. — Beyond Good and Evil, Friedrich Nietzsche

DARWIN proposed that evolution proceeded by both *natural* selection and *sexual* selection. The tenets of natural selection have been exhaustively studied for more than a century, and we assume the reader has at least a passing acquaintance with this subject. In contrast, the formal study of evolution driven by *sexual* selection, especially in humans, has been virtually ignored, possibly due to social prudery with respect to the subject of sex. Sex is a messy business after all. The result of such research could be personally unsettling and socially risky.

Nevertheless, the problem of "sex" remains.

Why sex evolved is especially problematic.[1] It turns out that attempting to explain mating behavior simply by means of survival is too naive, resulting in theories showing that asexual reproduction is more advantageous. Clearly, such theories are in error! Thus Darwin's distinction between natural selection and sexual selection must be reconsidered.

Our interest in the "why" of sex results from curiosity, whether or not our experience and observation of the courtship and mating behavior of a wide variety of women support the tenets of evolutionary psychology in general, and sexual selection in particular.

Furthermore, we see no hard distinction between the *biological* and the *psychological* aspects of the human being, but we consider them both as expressions of a whole. If you, the reader, are mystified in the matter of female relationships, some of the material we present in this book may seem to you to be very far from reality. However, when you observe the principles *in action*, you will begin to understand that female behavior and female psychology are both perfectly understandable.

[1] The "how" of sex, that swapping of genetic material, is well-understood.

This chapter will help you to understand some of the foundational psychological principles upon which male-female relationships are played out on a more biological and behavioral level in real life. These principles help explain a wide range of female behavior we discuss through the book. We'll start with sexual selection, then discuss evolutionary psychology, and close with some important points about altruism and selfishness as defined from an evolutionary perspective.

Sexual Selection

Selection refers to heritable traits that remain in — and have spread through — a population, because those traits served to increase the rate of reproduction of the organisms embodying those traits. *Heritability* refers to genetically-determined traits, which vary in their expression within a population. For example, we will refer to the female's manipulative skills, her degree of sexual desire, her mate-selecting skills, and so on. *Variation* refers to a state in which there exists a variety of genetically-determined traits within a population.

Sexual Selection can be divided into two main categories: *inter*-sexual selection, representing choices made with the opposite sex, and *intra*-sexual selection, representing choices made with respect to competition with the same sex.

Inter-sexual selection refers to the traits that one sex generally prefers in the opposite sex, such as leadership qualities, big muscles, impudence, aggressive behavior, and so on. (See Chapter 19, "Male Qualities Attractive to Women" for some practical tips on how to cultivate some of these key attributes within yourself). For example, a woman of a lower social level can easily identify survival with the skills for physical work at home, and she therefore may prefer a man who possess good skills for physical labour. A woman of a higher social level, on the other hand, may identify survival more with leadership qualities and impudence, and therefore may prefer a man who is able to put himself in the position of being the leader of other men.

Intra-sexual selection refers to competition occurring among the members of the *same* sex for mating access to the opposite sex. For example, it has been observed that a woman's sexual arousal can increase when she becomes aware that she is in the presence of a man who is sexually attractive to women *in general*. In other words, men who are successful with women tend to naturally attract more women to them *merely as a result* of their being attractive to other women. What is happening in this case is that the female evolutionary system has detected the man as being *fitter* for survival, and the female consequently reacts with increased sexual desire.

Evolutionary Psychology

Evolutionary psychology proposes that the human brain comprises many functional mechanisms called "psychological adaptations" or "evolved cognitive mechanisms," all evolving from natural or sexual selection. Some examples include: language acquisition modules, incest avoidance mechanisms, cheater detection mechanisms, intelligence and sex-specific mating preferences, foraging mechanisms, alliance-tracking mechanisms, agent detection mechanisms, and so on. We won't get into too much detail about each of those mechanisms, and will limit our discussion to:

- female sexuality and female emotional life, and
- female reproductive mechanisms from the point of view of sexual selection.

In general, evolutionary psychology asserts that many universal behaviors and aspects of society result from evolutionary adaptations. Such behaviors are studied to determine whether they are preserved in evolution as being useful to survival, or deleted for not being useful. For example, when we refer to females with high sexual drive or to females with low sexual drive, we are referring to sub-groups of women whose *baseline* sexual drive has evolved differently, depending on different survival needs and behaviors.

Within the framework of evolutionary psychology, a woman with a high sex drive is more prone to get impregnated by different men, which shifts her focus from the care of one child to the care of many children. Depending on her behavior with respect to social norms, such a woman may be labeled "promiscuous" or worse, "slutty." A woman with a low sex drive is less prone to be impregnated by many different men. Her focus is more on the care of fewer children than on her being impregnated by many men. Again, depending on her behavior, such a woman may be labeled "cold," or "frigid." Both high sex drive and low sex drive females are useful to nature for different reasons. In the first case, wider genetic variety results. In the second case, greater genetic survivability results.

Interestingly, these natural differences have been distorted by men, in an attempt to understand them and to cope with the fear caused by them. We believe that male cognitive distortion of these natural feminine traits is the reason for such beliefs within our modern population as the "Madonna/whore complex," which we discuss extensively later in the book, along with many other examples such as the so-called "last-minute resistance" and "anti-slut defense."

Altruism and Selfishness

Many men, especially men who have become emasculated by women, fail to understand the real evolutionary meaning of female altruism and/or selfishness, which truly *depends on the circumstances*. They fail to see it as a continuously changing process that occurs within the same woman, and instead they tend view it in a more static and conflictual way. We believe that under the influence of the Madonna/whore complex, men stereotypically categorize women into rigid categories of *altruistic* or *selfish*. This is understandable, because some of the mechanisms which are useful to the continuation of life and the fitness of the species are often very immoral and shocking when seen from the point of view of the individual. But this is the way it is.

Usually, women are naturally altruistic towards their children, and to a lesser extent, close family members. But what about a woman's interactions with men that she has romantic or sexual relationships with? Should you be expecting mercy or altruism towards you from your female romantic partners? Perhaps, perhaps not. Our belief is that it's never appropriate for a man to *expect* altruism from a woman, only to appreciate a woman's altruism when she provides it.

Men who become physically unfit in relationships learn very quickly that many woman have no compunction against kicking a man while he is down. As David says, she needs to *feel* that he is the same strong bastard she was initially attracted to, even when he is sick-in-bed with the flu. This is a purely selfish response from the woman for evaluating — on an emotional level — the man's continued fitness.

Consider the predicament suffered by the physically large, menacing Icelandic berserker Egil Skallagrimson. The onset of ill health (probably Paget's disease[2]) gradually rendered him deaf, blind and subject to migraines, whence, as the saga tells us, he was ridiculed by the women of his household, the same women he protected and provided for in his younger, healthier days![3]

> Egil, after moving in with his son-in-law, Grim, at Mosfell, was walking outside one day when he stumbled and fell. Some of the women who saw this laughed:
>
> "You're really finished, now, Egil," they said, "when you fall without being pushed."
>
> "The women didn't laugh so much when we were younger," said Grim.

[2]http://www.viking.ucla.edu/Scientific_American/Egils_Bones.htm
[3]*The Sagas of Icelanders*

It's to Egil's credit he eventually expired of old age, rather than the treachery or mischief rampant in Iceland during the periods of the sagas.

Among humans, altruism can be observed when comparing a woman from a more traditional, patriarchal country, to a woman from a more politically-correct, industrialized country. A woman of a traditional patriarchal country will be more motivated in terms of altruistic behavior towards her husband (that is, the family's *Provider*) because the role of family and patriarchy is still seen as much more important in those countries. In fact, supporting her man by sacrificing herself will increase the likelihood of spreading her own genes to her children.

This altruistic effect is virtually lost in politically-correct western countries, such that a woman's motivation for altruistic behavior towards her husband (Provider) may be almost nonexistent, or will be limited to a short period of time between getting pregnant to the early years of the infant's upbringing. Selfishness emerges when the woman can induce a man to pay for the children without impinging on her freedom, via the state-sanctioned mechanism of child support. This selfishness provides the woman with material support for children by one man, while allowing her to become impregnated by another man, with little or no material or social risk to herself.

In short, evolutionarily-derived altruism and selfishness both have clear reproductive advantages, depending on the woman's material and social circumstances. A practical man will keep these notions in mind when arranging his affairs with the woman or women in his life.

Practical Advice

It's not mandatory to accept all of the tenets of evolutionary psychology in order to be successful with women. However, such a study will broaden your understanding of why females think and act the way that they do. Three books we have found very helpful are Matt Ridley's *The Red Queen*, Robin Baker's

Sperm Wars and Geoffrey Miller's *The Mating Mind.* Each of these books are written by an expert in their field; brief reviews of each follow, below.

One of the defining books on the evolution of sexuality is *The Red Queen* by Ridley [1]. The author puts forth several theories as to why men feel compelled to ask a woman's hand in marriage and how we get our concepts of physical beauty, among many others. Ridley also presents a convincing array of statistics which seem to prove that a woman is more likely to be impregnated during an illicit affair than she is with her husband or long-term boyfriend. *The Red Queen* is fun read, and Ridley wrote it in an easily-accessible style that anyone new to the field of evolutionary psychology can readily grasp and enjoy. We therefore highly recommend *The Red Queen* to help round out your education.

Baker's *Sperm Wars* [2] is another extremely interesting book examining human reproductive strategy. Baker makes a case based on evolutionary biology that human males and females exhibit a wide range of sexual behavior as an evolutionary response for widening the gene pool. His treatment is explicit — at times *graphic* — in it's description of mating strategies, and he pulls no punches with respect to controversial topics, or even criminal behavior on the part of either males or females. As troubling as many of the behaviors Baker documents are, we find that fitting such behaviors into a rational and naturally-evolved framework is extremely helpful for guiding our interactions with women (and men).

Miller, an evolutionary psychologist at the London School of Economics and at UCLA, proposes in *The Mating Mind* [3] that a large portion of the human brain evolved into a *Courtship Mind* (the "mating mind"). This explains why many genetic traits such as talents for music, or mathematics, or mechanics — which have very poor value from the point of view of natural selection — have evolved in our species. Miller maintains that both sexes have evolved many significant ways of displaying fitness via expression of creative intelligence, such as story-telling, poetry, art, music, sport, dance, humour, kindness and leadership. That such traits not strictly connected with survival is problematic in other theories.

As we wrote in the introduction, this book is not intended to be a scientific textbook. Our main goals are to entertain and inform, and hopefully inspire men to action in creating the relationships that they desire with women. The interpretations given to the scientific literature cited are purely subjective and constitute the authors' own experiences with a wide variety of women and their interpretations of the studies. The validity of our interpretations should be confirmed or negated by concretely testing them in the field of male-female relationships.

Our experience, however, is our own. We're positive that if men test our theories within the realm of everyday experience with women, they will find them to be extremely practical. We encourage you to maintain an open mind, to read the books reviewed above, and to read more on this topic from the variety of sources found in the bibliography.

2 Female Neuropsychology

Perhaps truth is a woman who has reasons for not letting us see her reasons? — The Gay Science, Friedrich Nietzsche.

NEUROPSYCHOLOGY is the study of how the function and structure of the brain relates to specific psychological processes. Part of neuropsychology involves studying how brain activity expresses itself through verbal, cognitive and physical indicators. For example, with regards to sexuality and emotional life, there have been recent studies on the effects of childhood abuse on the neuropsychological and cognitive functions in women, and the effects of hormonal activity on sexual orientation.[1]

For centuries, women have been more advanced in knowledge of *male* sexual neuropsychology; women needed such skills for physical survival in a world dominated by large, aggressive men. Women are usually totally silent about their deep knowledge of the male psyche and sexuality. We believe this silence is a result of:

1. The female need to manipulate the male into a Provider role for reasons of survival.

2. The female need for social acceptance, or social status preservation when promiscuity is punished (this refers to the Madonna/whore Complex, which is extensively discussed later in the book).

Our particular interest in neuropsychology is on signs of female sexual arousal which can be detected by having a normal conversation with a woman, without the need to physically escalate the interaction towards a sexual act.[2] Sexual escalation

[1]We would like to see the subject of Female Neuropsychology taught to men at school! Many marriages would be saved and many couples would be happier.

[2]Since this is not a book about sexology, we will not be discussing subjects such as the female orgasm, or difficulties with orgasm.

is defined as the sequence of acts which bring a couple closer to the act of lovemaking. Understanding how to detect the level of female arousal without escalating physically increases a man's social awareness, allowing the interaction to proceed *covertly* rather than *overtly*. Since there exists a complex of verbal and non-verbal signs which indicate that the female is becoming sexually aroused, this is a skill: a woman's arousal is expressed through her body and her brain's cognitive activity in ways that can be detected by simple observation.

This concept of detecting female arousal through observation has been taboo for many centuries, we believe partly due to the Madonna/whore Complex and partly because we are only now beginning to understand the connection between brain activity and verbal and non-verbal signals. Due to the effect on the scientific media of the Madonna/whore Complex, a search of scientific literature on the topic of female sexual arousal finds studies about the "abnormalities" of female sexuality. There are very few articles on how a woman's sexual arousal can be detected in the context of normal, everyday social interactions.

Language and Female Sexual Arousal

Normal, healthy, adult women often become sexually aroused by *words* and *communication*. In neuropsychological terms, sexual arousal in women goes like this: *words* and *communication* and their effect on the woman's inner mental process creates a fantasy for her, and from this primary process follows the biological signs of sexual arousal, such as vaginal lubrication. Words and communication and their effect on the woman's inner mental process create pleasurable emotions, and from this primary process follows the biological signs of sexual arousal, for example an increase in her libido.

The emotions which cause sexual pleasure within a woman can be both *positive*, as in joy, or *negative*, as in fear or anger. We postulate that a woman who is routinely sexually aroused by negative emotions is almost definitely a woman with psychological problems and a woman with lower self-esteem (LSE — explained in depth later in the book). We also postulate that to a certain extent *all* women are sexually aroused by *strong* emotions, and that strong emotions can also include those that we would consider as "negative emotions", even within a psychologically healthy woman.

Female Need for Communication

Though females may train themselves to act like men, in reality they have a very deep biological urge to be talkative. Certain studies indicate that females get a rush of pleasure by certain hormones when talking. Female hormones seem to act in such a way so as to induce in the female an extreme need for emotional expression and talking with her peers.

It seems likely that men and women have difficulties in communication because the language they use and the needs they have with regards to their communication are often very different. Science has not been able to demonstrate this for sure but several studies seem to indicate that what is intended as "communication" may be something totally different for men and for women.

It is possible that already at the age of eighteen weeks, pregnancy hormones define a totally different structure of the brain in regards to what is intended as communication. In other words, sexual hormones may effect the parts of the male and female brain dedicated to communication, such that their neuropsychological expression may be totally different depending on whether the person is a male or female.

Mutual Gazing

There is a need for the female of our species to seek mutual gazing, or deep and prolonged eye contact. In our extensive field experience we have repeatedly noticed this to be true.

When a female is deprived of mutual gazing she gets anxious and depressed. Conversely, when she is rewarded by mutual gazing she gets pleasure and is satisfied. You might have noticed that your wife or girlfriend will become increasingly agitated when your eyes are focussed intently for any length of time on a television sporting event or towards your computer screen.

Our field experience also indicates that females have ambivalent feelings in regard to males who reward them by talking a lot and engaging in mutual gazing. On one hand, they feel happy and rewarded. On the other hand, in the long run, women will react with a decrease in sexual attraction towards the male who seeks *too much* attention from women in this way.

Our rationale for this is that sexual attraction is created by contrast. Ultimately, females are attracted by masculine features. Therefore, men who reward females with a lot of feminine traits such as conversation and mutual gazing are at risk of having those females lose attraction for them in the long run. These men risk becoming too effeminate in the eyes of their women. Calibration is therefore crucial; you will need to listen and observe and thereby determine the right amount of these things.

Female Blueprint

A Female Blueprint is a specific set of emotions which is individual to the particular woman and which elicits sexual arousal in her when it is targeted — either consciously or unconsciously — by the male. The Blueprint has an evolutionary purpose: it sets the conditions for specific evolutionary selection based on certain specific features, which are by nature much more specific than what would arouse most males. Males, as we all know, can be easily aroused by the sight of a naked, beautiful woman. But female arousal is not usually as simple as that.

Here are some typical Female Blueprints:

- A woman is sexually aroused by successful businessmen who cause her to daydream about flying worldwide for the purpose of building successful businesses. As you can see, this is very specific, and the woman will predictably become sexually aroused by men who elicit this Blueprint from her. She may be totally incapable of sexual arousal with a guy who is of the "rock star" type and without good business sense.
- A woman is sexually aroused by men who give her the feeling of being free and wild; for example, in the manner that a rock star or a member of a motorcycle gang might do. In this case, she will remain completely cold sexually when in the company of a businessman and will show biological signs of sexual arousal when in the presence of the rock star.
- A woman is sexually aroused by the emotions created by going shopping and looking for red underwear for herself, especially if this happens in the company of a man who is able to describe with *words* the features of these clothes. We'll have more to say about such language, which we call *Rich Description*.

As you can see, female sexual arousal has much wider variability when compared with male sexuality.

Passivity and Receptiveness

Passivity and Receptiveness are essential states that the average woman needs to get into in order to become aroused sexually. A truly feminine woman will find it difficult to become sexually aroused with a man unless he is able to make her comfortable with being both *passive* and *receptive* to the man and his advances. If a woman indicates that she becomes aroused by acting tough, by fighting or by primarily visual means, similar to a man, we can say that her *masculine* behavior has either been learned or is intrinsic to her nature for biological reasons.

Body Language and Sexual Arousal

It would be almost impossible to list and describe all of the potential signs of female sexual arousal. We provide a few key examples in order to give you an overview of the correlation between the psychology of a woman and the neuropsychological expression of her arousal.

Soft Signs are expressions visible through body language and through cognitive brain activity that something is happening within the brain. What follows is a list of some Soft Signs indicating female sexual arousal. This list could be very lengthy, especially for an experienced seducer:

1. Looking downward after having had eye contact with a male she is sexually attracted to is a clear sign of submission among all primates.
2. Giggling is often sign of submissiveness.
3. Emotional or dramatic outbursts. In most cases, this is a clear sign of sexual arousal in a woman.
4. Impaired concentration and an increase in the unrelatedness of emotions within a sequence.
5. An increase in lower body movements which attract male attention.
6. Blushing.
7. Scratching of her wrists and inner arms.

Practical Advice

All of our work in this book is based on the assumption that the human being is a cybernetic system wherein the mind and body are inseparable parts of the same system and affect each other. In other words, we believe that the mind and the body of a person are closely coupled, rendering true distinctions difficult to determine.

You are now in a position to train yourself to observe the soft signs of arousal within your woman. You will find a clear correlation with what you do — and what you do not do — in the course of your relationship and the signs of her arousal. Learn to *calibrate*. Keep in mind that the main purpose of evolution is to screen for better genes and that everything that your woman does or doesn't do is in one way or another linked to that purpose.

There are couple of very good guidebooks with respect to Soft Signs available in the mainstream literature. Leil Lowndes' *Undercover Sex Signals* [4] is a compendium of just such mannerisms as listed above, and many, many more. Ms. Lowndes is an outstanding author, perceptively noting that such signals should not be taken at face value. Rather, view each soft sign as a "letter". By learning to assemble these "letters", you become adept at reading her "words", which in turn are communicating her intentions.

Tracey Cox's *Superflirt* [5] could be considered an illustrated encyclopedia of body language. Some of the material is similar in content to *Undercover Sex Signals*, but the presentation is complementary. We recommend that you get both books.

3 Female Logic Explained

I want wonderful and fascinating and marvelous things to happen to me and I don't want to do anything to make them happen. Nothing at all. —Lanya, from *Dhalgren*, by Samuel R. Delany

FOR ages, men have considered "Female Logic," or the female way of thinking, to be one of the greatest mysteries in the universe. Psychoanalysts, philosophers and poets have spent countless amounts of time agonizing over this topic.

Well, the good news is that female logic (also known as *chick logic*) can be explained to men in a perfectly understandable way. You can learn how female logic works just like you can learn the functions of a computer or the technical specifications of a car.

First of all, based on what we considered in Chapter 1 with regards to Evolutionary Psychology, let's stipulate that every function of the human brain has an evolutionary purpose. The evolutionary purpose of female logic is to achieve two basic goals:

1. To create ideal conditions for the procreation and birth of children, and ideal conditions to protect those children during their early years of development.

2. To influence the men and the environment around her to give her and her children support and protection. This influence commonly manifests as manipulation (more about manipulation in Chapter 13), which in this scenario may be seen as a positive force used by the woman instinctually as a means to support life.

A woman naturally achieves these goals by creating within herself a sense of emotional congruence. When creating such emotions, the woman is especially concerned with "how she feels right now" as opposed to a male-logic concern of "how *a* correlates to *b*, or how *a* is the cause of *b*." In psychologically healthy women, these will be emotions of pleasure and safety. In other women, drama, histrionics and hysteria serve a similar purpose.

In the following discussion, the reader should keep in mind we are not making any value or moral judgments. Emotional reasoning is very likely deeply embedded into people, if not all mammals. Human males have simply evolved a further characteristic of being more able to easily suppress emotional reasoning.[1]

The Calculus of Emotion

Female logic is based on a *calculus of emotion*, allowing a woman to understand her current emotional state as a causal result of a chain of external factors. *That these factors may be physically illogical or irrational is emotionally irrelevant*. Men typically have a great deal of trouble following women's physically non-causal emotional reasoning, and don't understand that to the woman, accepting the emotion is much more important than determining a logical or rational underlying cause.

Female logic can be visualized as a sequence of emotional states along of the lines of the imaginary chain:

$$\ldots \to b \to c \to x \to y \to z \to u \to a \to b \to \ldots$$

where the elements are absolutely not required to be in what men would consider logical, rational or physically causal correlation between each other. Instead, these states are correlated in terms of how the emotion b was the cause within the woman of the emotion c, and of the emotion x and so on, without any other correlation between each of the other elements whatsoever, and where there is no certainty about which element may or may not be the cause of the next one in the sequence.

Note: we are making some very broad generalizations here!

[1]Men who manipulate women often turn tables on women by employing this same sort of reasoning. The authors view this as an abrogation of masculinity: men should lead, not manipulate.

Some women employ chick logic exclusively, other women not so much. But in our experience, most women will resort to emotional reasoning when under the influence of powerful, uncomfortable emotional states, or in uncomfortable social circumstances.

Some women's behavior is primarily driven by their emotions. In many cases, these women share their feelings with you in a balanced way, having developed very good control over their emotions. In other cases women can be prone to discharge their problems on you in a massive way. Neither one of these types of women may have a functioning sense of causality between her emotional states. Trying to apply male logic to women and their emotional states is therefore inappropriate and it only leads to frustration in the male attempting the analysis.

It is important to note that female emotionality is of an *inward* nature. Franco believes this is strictly connected with pregnancy and motherhood. This may appear in some women as extreme self-centeredness. In reality this trait is a positive strength created by nature to achieve maximum well-being in a woman's body and in her psyche, in preparation for the creation of a new life. It may sometimes seem to you that your woman is unable to feel empathy towards your needs as a man. For this reason it is crucial for a Modern Man to be totally *nonneedy* in any relationship with a woman.

Biological and Psychological Factors

We believe sex drive and self-esteem both influence a woman's susceptibility to use emotional calculus.

Women with a High Sex Drive, defined as "HD" in this book (details in Chapter 7), exhibit female logic to a more impressive extent. This is because female logic is not an isolated phenomenon, but it is strictly connected with the woman's sexual instinct. In contrast, women with a Lower Sex Drive, defined in this book as "LD", exhibit female logic to a lesser degree. The Modern Man *can* use seduction techniques to change LD women into HD women, if he so chooses. When that happens, the formerly-LD woman starts to exhibit emotional thinking to a greater extent than before.

LD women also use female logic, but it is different compared with the female logic displayed by HD women and it is also more *subtle*.

Self-esteem is another factor which influences female logic to a great degree. Women with Low Self-Esteem (defined in this book as "LSE"), employ a more primitive, wilder kind of female logic. Women with High Self-Esteem (defined in this book as "HSE") have a higher-level kind of female logic, which is detectable only by very experienced seducers. Most men will be able to notice female logic coming from an LSE woman, but they will rarely be able to detect female logic coming from an HSE woman.

Emotional Awareness

Most men would like to relax when they get into a committed relationship with a woman. In an attempt to relax, the man will start an attempt to establish *control her behavior* as soon as he gets in touch with her emotional side. This almost always leads to disappointment, because often a woman will dramatically escalate her use of female logic the more she is sexually attracted to her man. The more logic and control a man attempts to establish, the more the woman will escalate emotionally. For her, it's a matter of self-defense to preserve her sense of identity as a woman.

When a man tries to have his woman's female logic repressed and transformed into male logic, he may actually be repressing his woman's sexual attraction towards him. It is vital to remember that the kind of emotional thinking within the woman — which we identify as female logic — may be strongly linked to her sexuality.

Dealing with a woman and her female logic in the proper way

is not difficult, but you cannot relax in the way a man normally intends to relax. This is because if a man could naturally understand a woman when she is thinking with her female logic, he would no longer be a real man, but rather quite an effeminate man. Instead, to make a woman happy and sexually active, a man must cultivate a constant state of awareness within himself: be aware of *her* emotional state, without allowing her emotional state to affect *you*.

So the key to dealing with female logic is *constant emotional awareness*. In fact, you can bet that without being emotionally awareness your woman will surprise you, sometimes in very unpleasant ways, and on a regular basis. With emotional awareness, you will be able to anticipate her emotions, and lead her through a sequence of positive states.

Practical Advice

The best way to deal with female logic is to help your woman to actually *enhance* it, instead of trying to change her. This must happen in such a way that you never lose your masculine frame, because if you do that then you will become her "male girlfriend"; emotionally close for sure, but without the sexual tension that is at the very center of any healthy romantic relationship.

At its core, female logic is somewhat schizophrenic. Therefore, in order to be able to deal with it successfully, you have to position yourself in a little bit of a schizophrenic manner; i.e. you must be able to talk *chickspeak*, without ever losing the sexually active and aggressive frame of the masculine male.

The big problem with books such as John Gray's "Men are From Mars, Women are From Venus" [6] is that while they can help men to understand female logic to a certain degree, in the process they emasculate the man, stripping him of his masculine core. In order to maintain sexual attraction from a female, we need to *understand* female logic but at the same time remain as *real, masculine men*. We do not effectively resolve the differences between male logic and female logic by becoming females!

An important thing for the modern man to keep in mind is that the mechanism of female logic is especially activated by the presence of the male himself. The more a woman finds herself in the presence of a masculine man, and especially if she is sexually attracted to that man, the more she will get into the emotional mental state described above.

Flip the Script

The rationalization by women of their emotional processes is what we like to call "Chick Logic" and it is a fundamental weapon in the female arsenal for managing their relationships with men. Chick logic leads to notions such as "If you don't talk about it, it never happened." When you hear a phrase like this from a woman, understand that what this means in practice is that she doesn't want to talk about something that "causes" her to *feel bad*. Never mind whether the whole incident was captured on video, that's completely irrelevant to her. As long as she never talks about it, she never has to feel those bad emotions.[2]

When a man gets angry with a woman and describes her as a "selfish bitch," what is happening is that he is relating to a woman who is presently focused, to an extreme extent, on how she feels *right now*. In fact, the more a woman can be referred to in the context of male logic as a "bitch", the stronger and more primitive her female sexual instinct is.

Women exhibit female logic to different degrees. The degree to which a woman exhibits female logic is caused by biological, psychological and social factors.

[2] DAVID remembers that he had a relationship once with a woman who came back from a small resort 90 miles south of Cancún and let the following comment slip: "What happens in the islands stays in the islands." At that time, he didn't think much of it. Now, it strikes him that she probably had sex while she was down there, and didn't want to feel guilty for "cheating."

Some In-Field Examples of Female Logic

Franco has been married twice and has otherwise been in loving relationships with many women. Once upon a time he picked up a woman. Let's call her Lady BadKisser. This girl was at that time looking for a committed relationship and Franco was enjoying being single. As usual, Franco attempted to initiate sex with the woman. It is our very strong opinion that no man should even think about starting a serious relationship with a woman if she does not demonstrate from the outset that she enjoys being sexually engaged with the man.

So, Lady BadKisser kissed Franco, but when he kissed her, he could sense that she was reacting with uneasiness to his kiss. This was a good indication to Franco that he should forget this particular woman and concentrate on the next one. So Franco naturally reduced his time with her. On a subsequent occasion the woman told Franco that the reason for her hesitancy was because Franco was not willing to have a serious relationship, which was quite true at that time.

After that, they did not meet again for several years. In the meantime, Franco got married again, and while Franco was married, he met up with Lady BadKisser. They talked and they had quite a good time together, and wouldn't you know it? She tried to kiss Franco. After that, she started to call him and to send him text messages quite frequently.

This woman was clearly an LD woman and Franco was quite interested in understanding how it was that she had this apparent sudden change from LD to HD. She was actually embarrassing him, by being quite sexually aggressive towards him all the time while they were out together in public.

Well, when finally they talked in depth about this, Franco found out the reason:

Lady BadKisser: "Franco, you are a married man now, so I finally know that I can trust you."

Unbelievable!

In fact, this story makes perfect sense when viewed in the light of female logic. The woman did not trust Franco when he was single. She believed that Franco was only interested in a casual, sexual relationship with her. At that time, under the influence of her strong emotional state "X", she was unable to see that Franco *may* be capable of a committed relationship *in the future*. To do that she would have had to be capable of stepping out of her emotional state and thinking logically.

When she came to know that Franco was now married, she came under the influence of another, different emotional state, let's call it State "Y", which for her means, "I can trust this guy, because he can be my husband". This new emotional state confused her logic even more because she started to *feel* that *she* should be Franco's wife and not some other woman.

When we analyze this woman's contrasting emotional states "X" and "Y," we see that she is not capable of logically connecting the two states together. For her, the two states are equally real and equally valid, except that state "X" no longer applies, because it is now evident that Franco is *husband material*, which corresponds to her desires for a man, and not a bachelor, which is unattractive to her.[3]

Lead Her Emotions

The authors can deliberately induce an emotional, feminine-logic state in women. We have seduced somewhat-masculine women, those being defined as women who have consciously trained themselves to suppress their female logic. Here are a few real-life examples:

Woman: "Franco, I had believed that I was not a chicken like my mother is, but when I am with you I feel I am just like her."
... or ...
Woman (shouting): "I am used to being in control!"
... or ...
Woman: "Unbelievable!... I do not feel ashamed about sex at all when I am with you."

[3]Women can learn to logically connect with their emotional states. Apparently, this is as difficult for women as emotionally connecting to logical states is to a man.

And so on.

The vast majority of men are totally unaware of how their own close proximity to their women is the actual *cause* of the woman going deeper and deeper into this natural emotional state. Once you acknowledge this fact, a lot of good things will start to happen for you. For one thing, you no longer need to argue or have fights with your woman!

The majority of arguing that occurs among couples is in fact due to men attempting to apply male logic to women, and women trying to apply their female logic to men, while they are interacting with each other. Therefore, if you want to increase the sexual attraction of a woman and communicate with her effectively, stop asking her the following type of question when she is in an emotional state: "How the hell does X relate to Y? Or how does Y relate to Z?"

For example, she may shift from an emotion called X to an emotion called Y during your conversation, without any apparent logical connection between the two points. You need to understand that the only logical connection between the two points is definitely something in her outer world, which has caused her to shift from the emotion X to the emotion Y.

Here is another real-life example:

Franco: "So tonight we are going to watch a wonderful movie.. Yesterday when we spoke, we agreed to go at 5:00PM."
Woman: "Where are you?"
Franco: "At the office. So I will meet you at the railway station at 4:45 pm. They say this war movie is very good."
Woman: "You are always working. You surely like to be away from home!"

At this point, she is clearly feeling some strong emotions connected with Franco being at the office. Unfortunately, the majority of men would react like this:

Average Guy, in an angry or frustrated tone: "Hey look! I have my next client about to come in. So are we going to meet at 4:45

or not?"

This response would be a very logical thing to do, because the man surely remembers that in the morning they had agreed to go to watch that movie together. However, this would be a case of trying to apply male logic to the woman's emotional state. She will likely be upset by such a response and feel that her man doesn't understand her. Instead, the experienced seducer would drop the logical, male reaction and instead respond with something like this:

Franco: "Yes.. to think if I would have to go and fight in a war... so many months away from home."
Woman: "You enjoy killing, don't you?!?"
Franco: "I sure do love the feeling of running towards the enemy and putting a bullet into his head."

Here Franco shows that he does not care too much about her disappointment, but this causes no problem because Franco is in fact matching her emotional state in that moment. That, in fact, is what women want! Imagine that this discussion continues as follows:

Woman: "All men are the same; they only want money, power, and killing!"
Franco: "Yes. Actually I think we should purify ourselves... how about we plan our next vacation for the monastery at Valamo?"

And on and on he goes, teasing her about her emotions, and as a result she gets hornier and hornier. Franco missed out on going to many movies in this way!

Meta-emotions

Culturally, the West has placed a premium on male control of emotions, which is nearly always performed by using rational logic. We believe that both men and women experience the same suite of emotions to a greater or lesser degree. A man can develop the ability to tap into emotions just as women do.

Once a man is attuned to a woman's base emotions, he is able to tune into much deeper emotional states. For example, consider the following statement: "Sometimes, it feels good to feel bad." Most men have absolutely no conception of what such an obviously contradictory statement means.

And most women do.

Furthermore, even men who understand the concepts of contradictory emotional states in an intellectual way, may remain completely unable to enjoy these emotions with women. In the worst case, a man will treat woman's capability to enjoy contradictory and conflicting emotions with contempt.

One common way to gain an understanding of meta-emotions is to ask a women how she feels about how she feels. Suppose she is feeling good about something. Does she feel good about feeling good? Or does she feel bad about feeling good.

4 Female Basic Conflict

Tell me, what you're thinking about
When you got me waiting patiently
Usually, I don't have to wait for nobody
But there's something about you
That really got me feeling weak
— *Tell Me,* by P. Diddy (feat. Christina Aguilera)

TRULY understanding the psychology of women requires being aware of a fundamental conflict in the nature of women's relationships with men: women are more sexually attracted to men who are less inclined to provide for them. That is, in their hearts chicks love to love *bad boys*, but in their heads they know that *nice guys* make much better husbands.

This Female Basic Conflict is a schizophrenic duality between a woman's need for survival, on the one hand, and her need to express her own sexuality, on the other. This creates a psychological condition whereby a woman's sexuality is necessarily ambivalent and conflicted, in order to be able express itself to the maximum extent. In this chapter we will help you to easily recognize this phenomenon in women and how to deal with it effectively.

In a nutshell, the Female Basic Conflict is:

- The need to manipulate a man into the role of her *Provider*.
- Automatic contempt and a lowering of her sexual attraction towards a man who lets her do so.

The Lover-Provider Dichotomy

Before we discuss the Female Basic Conflict in depth, we need to provide you with an explanation of certain terms. Throughout history, women have typically been condemned for any expression of their natural sexuality. In addition, women have naturally a strong survival instinct, which is intrinsically tied in with pregnancy and child care. Because of these two factors, women have developed a strong tendency to divide men into one of two categories: *Lover* or *Provider*.

The Lover

The *Lover* is a man with whom a woman can freely express her sexuality, without having to be worried about that man attempting to exert control over her — either in a physical way or with respect to her material well-being — and without having to be worried about being morally judged by that man.

In our modern society, a woman will typically consider a man a Lover, only if he is not in a position of having any responsibility for her or her children, and only if he does not live in the same *territory* as her (i.e., he does not share a house or apartment with her), nor exerts any physical or material power over her. At the same time, the Lover induces a strong sexual attraction within the woman.

The Provider

A *Provider*, on the other hand, can be defined as a man who has agreed to take responsibility for the woman and her children, both financially and emotionally. This usually is accompanied by the exerting of power over the woman.

We will analyze the characteristics of men who are either Lovers or Providers throughout this book. At this time, suffice it to say that when a woman chooses a Lover, she is primarily basing this choice on an emotional basis, with respect to the raw sexual attraction she feels. An intelligent woman will usually only choose a man as a Provider after careful, rational analysis over a period of time. The conflict arises due to the fact that when a man positions himself in the Provider role, he will generally be perceived by the woman in such a way that her feelings towards him as a Lover are negated or at least diminished. This is due to the fact that, in many ways, the Lover personality is in conflict with the Provider personality.

The Lover-Provider dichotomy creates a psychological dissociation within the woman, which occurs mostly on the subconscious level.

For the modern man, it is essential to be able to discern the expression of this conflict, by reading the neuropsychological responses of the woman's brain activity and through an understanding of the role of evolution behind such behavior.

To be able to deal successfully with a woman's emotional life, you need to focus on the process, much more than any specific words being spoken, during any interaction with a woman.

You should also to be able to view the *relationship* with a woman as more of an *ongoing process*, rather than something static and stable. Men — who are normally very good at understanding processes — often make the big mistake of considering a relationship with a woman as something fixed, immovable, or permanent, especially once the couple has settled in to a more or less long-term type of relationship, or expressed words of commitment to each other.

This erroneous, predominantly male viewpoint only results in disappointment for both the man and the woman.

Dissociation

The Lover-Provider dichotomy often presents itself psychologically as an act of *dissociation* in women. This occurs so often due to the oppression of female sexuality throughout history. As a modern man you need to fully understand what is involved in the phenomenon known as dissociation. Dissociation is a state of acute mental decompensation in which certain thoughts, emotions, sensations, and/or memories are compartmentalized because they are too overwhelming for the conscious mind to integrate. An example of dissociation is this:

> Woman: (to her girlfriend or lover) "He is a good husband but I can't help but laugh at him for his niceness. He does all that I demand."

Unconsciously, what this woman is really saying is: I cannot feel sexual attraction for a man who is being a Provider to me because I know he does that because he cannot get women to be sexually submissive to him. So I need now a Lover who makes me feel like a woman again.

Many women may act like this in a totally innocent manner, not even aware of all of the psychological forces at work, because in their marriages with Providers they have felt they are under the effect of an oppression which has been put upon women for centuries.

Now as a man what you need to know is this: under the effect of the Lover-Provider dichotomy a woman can find herself in a totally dissociative state which, means that she can act out under the influence of strong emotions in seemingly unpredictable ways. In other words, you can expect just about anything.

Dangers of Being Strictly a Provider

As we discuss at length throughout this book, behaviors are both evolutionarily-determined as well as learned. The process of learning behaviors, however, is very slow. New human behaviors which fit better with survival can be learned and behaviors which become obsolete may be unlearned, but this takes a lot of time; often this process can take several generations.

In Western countries in the 21st Century we find ourselves in precisely such a situation. Women no longer have much of a practical *need* to manipulate a man into serving as a Provider to them, and women therefore find that they are struggling to unlearn these manipulative behaviors.

This is a very difficult process because on the one hand, such manipulative behavior can still be very fruitful to a woman in terms of survival in today's world, but on the other hand such behavior often brings internal and external conflict to the woman.

As a modern man you need to learn to be able to read this conflict in women *on the fly* as part of her ongoing, internal processes. You need to be able to objectively analyze this conflict on an ongoing basis as it occurs within the particular woman in front of you.

If a man tries to put himself strictly in the Provider role with a modern woman, sooner or later he will elicit in her the following symptoms:

- Boredom
- A massive lowering of her sexual attraction towards him
- In some cases, even outright contempt from her towards the man

You need to realize that the Provider frame is a dangerous frame to find yourself in nowadays. It has always been dangerous, but before, women were acting less dissociative than now. In the Modern Age the degree of dissociation coming from the Lover-Provider dichotomy is at its maximum. This is largely due to a culture which simultaneously grants women greater sexual freedom than ever before, while compelling men to provide materially for families that they may no longer form a strong part of, i.e. in cases of child custody disputes, child support payments, and alimony.

To keep up a woman's sexual attraction you have to be a *Lover* to her first and foremost. You can be also a Provider to her, but only without taking away the Lover part of your personality. As you read and absorb the information contained in this book, you are developing the tools you need to achieve that goal.

In today's modern society this can be quite a challenge. Young women are unfortunately often raised to view men as little better than sperm donors, fuck buddies or ATM machines. Young girls raised with an absence of fathers tend to view men in a love-hate fashion, and they tend to be quite mystified as to the psychological needs and desires of men, if they even care about that at all.

Consider the consequences on relationships with women subject to the Female Basic Conflict. Under the influence of this conflict a modern woman can and will give you contradictory communication, and she will do so on a *continuous* basis. It cannot be emphasized enough: a relationship with a woman should be viewed as a never-ending, *ongoing process*; not something that can be resolved once and for all.

Commitments, marriage, pronouncements of never-ending love made during romantic moments; none of these change the fact that a relationship with a woman is a never-ending process, and hopefully a happy process at that.

Female Projection

An important feature of female psychology is the projection of her emotions and needs into the environment. In other words, women tend to automatically place the responsibility for their emotions and needs on to their immediate environment. People with psychological education know that this is actually a trait of Borderline Personality Disorder. Obviously, the vast majority of women are do not suffer from Borderline Personality Disorder, but it is interesting that this trait is apparently a normal part of psychologically healthy women in a reduced sense.

Female Ambivalence

Ambivalence is defined as state of having emotions of both positive and negative valence or of having thoughts or actions in contradiction with each other, when they are related to the same object, idea or person (for example, simultaneously feeling both love and hatred for someone or something). The term is also commonly used to refer to situations where 'mixed feelings' of a more general sort are experienced or where a person experiences uncertainty or indecisiveness concerning something.

A woman will often assume the right of delivering mixed messages to you, without accepting any responsibility for doing so. In our modern society, this is in fact an extremely useful evolutionary trait for a woman to adopt, in terms of her survival.

The evolutionary positive gain for the woman from her use of Ambivalence is that she keeps her options open, and in this way she can gain advantages from as many sources as possible. For example, a woman will often achieve material advantage with a Provider and sexual pleasure with a Lover and successfully rule over both of them, if these men do not have the skills to deal with her manipulation.

Men are logical creatures. When they build relationships with females they tend to act along structures based on a logical sequence $a \rightarrow b \rightarrow c \rightarrow d \rightarrow e \rightarrow f \cdots$ and so on. When you create a structure you are doing something *yang* i.e. *masculine.*

The secret wish of every woman is: to find a man who is able to build a safe and strong masculine *yang* structure around her feminine *yin.*

For more on Female Ambivalence, please see Chapter 12 under the section "A/B Indecision".

Practical Advice

One of the standards you must adopt as a man, *in advance,* is to decide what role you would prefer to fulfill, with any woman you encounter. For example, if you are not interested in becoming a Provider, you will want to avoid behaviors that will tend to demonstrate that you are slotting yourself into the Provider role or that the woman can count on you for Provider-like behavior. For example, if you want to be strictly a Lover to a woman, it would be unwise to make a big display of showering her with free dinners and gifts, particularly before you have had repeated sexual relations with her.

Understand that women will unconsciously test, and test vigorously, and they will then slot you into either the Lover or

Provider category. For example, a woman may demand that you pay for her dinner or movie ticket, while reciting some commonly-used line such as "a gentleman always pays." This will not be a problem for you if you have already decided — well in advance — the type of man you are and what a woman can expect from her time with you.

If you are wavering on this point — if you say to yourself that you will have a policy of never paying for a woman but then buckle when confronted with a determined, sexually-hot female — you will invariably lose this game. A woman may or may not really prefer a man who pays for her, but she will always *despise* a man who is unsure of himself and his standards.

The challenge to you as a man lies within your ability to tolerate female ambivalence. If you can, you may succeed in becoming dominant over her, which can greatly increase the chances of her remaining sexually attracted to you and a generally happy relationship.

Your goal as a Modern Man should be to build a Yang *structure* for the relationship, while simultaneously being able to psychologically tolerate female ambivalence. In fact, the more feminine she is, the more she will tend to be and act ambivalent.

Unfortunately, the abdicating personal responsibility by women is widely promoted and condoned in western media culture and modern society. Therefore, as a Modern Man you need to learn to deal with this factor in real time and on an ongoing basis with the women you interact with. One way to do this is to set strong borders with a woman. This does *not* mean to become controlling or domineering. Controlling and manipulative behavior will automatically kill her perception of you as a Lover. It *does* mean having strong principles and standards that you adhere to and do not waver on, regardless of a woman's tears or how sexually desirable she appears to you.

5 Female Subcommunication

You should be stronger than me
Don't you know you supposed to be the man?
You always wanna talk it through - I don't care!
Why'd you always put me in control?
— *Stronger Than Me* by Amy Winehouse

ONE of the most important aspects to understand about female psychology is the use and existence of a type of language known as *subcommunication*. It is a secret language evolved by women over millennia in a male-dominated world. In this secret language women communicate their sexuality freely but in a way that most men cannot hear or understand. Women have learned the hard way through millennia that men have a psychological need to create a type of schizophrenic distinction among women, slotting all women into a category of either "whores" or "Madonnas".

Subcommunication is based on communicating with indirection, double meaning, ambiguity, emotionality and imprecision for the following purposes:

- To preserve social harmony.
- To avoid responsibility and establish plausible deniability.
- To signal intent, as in "Tell without telling, ask without asking."
- To establish boundaries and frames of interactions.
- To avoid commitment; maintain ambivalence; keep options open.

Furthermore, subcommunication *imposes upon the recipient* the responsibility of correctly interpreting the meaning.

In this chapter, we will focus on subcommunication within the context of female sexuality.

Basis for Subcommunication

Men, throughout history, have traditionally wanted to own women and women's bodies. In response, women had to invent a secret language that their oppressor could not understand, but that other women could easily understand.

Women protect themselves using subcommunication when direct communication is dangerous. For example, women can be quite promiscuous, yet the consequences for being promiscuous throughout history has often meant ostracism or even death for the woman, and humiliation for their families and the men that they are partnered with. No woman wants to be called a slut, which is exactly what happens even to *modern, western women* who are not sufficiently circumspect when discussing matters of female sexuality outside of trusted circles of friends.

As a result, while talking to each other and to men, women have learned to speak in this secret language. One of the purposes of this book is to disclose to men the secrets of Female Subcommunication, to be a translator of "womanese" to men. To be able to truly love a woman for who she is, a man must be able to read between the lines when it comes to her communication.[1]

In contrast to women, men practice more of a *direct* style of communication. Men approach subjects of conversation in a manner which is more straight-to-the-point. Women, on the other hand, prefer to subcommunicate.

Another reason for Female Subcommunication is the female preference for harmony of communication over absolute truth. The more feminine the woman, the more she will prefer harmony to the objective truth. On the other hand, what is intended as the truth in the masculine world is something which is usually said succinctly, directly and in synthetic way.

[1]Throughout this book, we will use the terms "womanese" and "subcommunication" interchangeably to refer to the female style of indirect — and often secret — conversation.

Men gain social power by penetrating the space around them, through logic and mathematics and via physical strength and endurance. Women gain social power by communication, and will often try to avoid, at all costs, any appearance of social conflict. Female Subcommuniation is especially used in order to achieve social power through manipulation of their social counterparts, such that their social counterparts are persuaded to give women what they want.

We can even observe biological reasons for the differences between female and male styles of communication. As we've already mentioned, the female brain seems to actually be structured differently than the male brain, in significant ways, and in particular when it comes to the processing of language. It can be observed on the neuropsychological level that female language is much more descriptive and rich, whereas male language tends to be much shorter and precise.

In a recent book called *The Female Brain* [7], Dr. Louann Brizendine claims that women actually devote more brain cells to talking than men do. Women actually get a chemical high from talking, and that would explain why they love to talk so much and why many men do not possess the same level of verbal com-munications skills that women do. While many of Brizendine's findings have been disputed and harshly criticized, we have no doubt that the average woman possesses a social intelligence that the average man cannot conceive of. With the knowledge we provide you with here, however, you will be able to un-derstand female communication on a whole new level, putting you in a category above and beyond the vast majority of men in the world.

From the point of view of most women, male communication is extremely poor and boring. For most men, female language is incredibly imprecise, infuriatingly vague and, when exposed to it for extended periods of time, becomes extremely stressful for the man. The end result is that it is a rare man indeed who is actually able to read between the lines of female communication. Typically, such a rare man will be a so-called "natural", or an experienced seducer.

Because of these differences, most men and women feel a great deal of dissatisfaction when it comes to their communication with the opposite sex. While we can certainly improve in our communication with each other, we can never eradicate these differences completely because they are largely determined by the different brain structures of men and women.

Most men go through life never even realizing that women subcommunicate. A lot of men are raised primarily by their mothers and they form a strong impression of women as either "Madonnas" or "whores," because of the strong social conditioning put into their heads by their mothers and society at large. There are also a group of strong alpha men who grow up with either a non-existent or very weak feminine side and for this reason they also end up with very little knowledge of women and the way women communicate.

In the latter group, we find men of great strength and value, such as military men or very successful businessmen. Ironically, these men may simultaneously become very emasculated within their relationships with their wives. These guys often sense that something strange is going on but they cannot pinpoint what it is. Often, out of frustration, such men will make the mistake of either completely cutting off communication with their partners, or perhaps even worse, taking everything their woman says at face value.

Phenomenology of Female Subcommunication

One of the core features of female subcommunication is *ambivalence*. One way to describe this is as "A/B Ambivalence", where the woman will leave open the possibility of either interpretation "A" or interpretation "B" with regards to her communication, without her taking any position either way. The woman may achieve this through open-ended statements, which leave the responsibility for interpreting the subject of communication with the recipient, with little help in regard to it from the communicator.

Evolutionarily, this approach to communication can be seen as good business for the woman, because she can protect herself via ambiguity while at the same time leaving the door open for a variety of different possible social interactions. The more effective a woman is at the art of subcommuniction the greater her social power. And as we've already mentioned, women achieve power in a distinctly *social* way.

To see further the difference in communication styles between men and women, consider the way each gender tends to deliver advice to friends of the same sex. For example, a masculine man will tend to give advice to his best friend regarding his alcohol problem, first by being silent for as long as possible, but then finally sitting down with his friend and saying: "Man, you are destroying your health, you gotta stop that drinking now!" without too much concern for empathy or understanding.

A woman in the same situation is unlikely to take a direct position about the drinking, but rather — taking an approach of subcommunication — she is more likely to show empathy and make an effort to understand her friend, in the hope that she will change.

Of course, as we know, both approaches are very likely to fail miserably if the person has a severe drinking problem, but it is always good to try. The illustration is merely meant to highlight the different approaches to communication generally taken by men and women.[2]

Effect of Subcommunication on the Male Brain

Female subcommunication has another very important role from the point of view of the survival of the species. It happens to be highly hypnotic to the male brain!

[2] The authors will use this in their seductions. They will temporarily give up the usage of male, logical language and will begin to subcommunicate meanings to women with open-ended statements. When this happens, women tend to feel: "Wow! A man who can really communicate!"

What has been described as romantic love by poets is actually — on the biological level — a strategy of nature designed to achieve pregnancy. A hypnotic state is basically a state of extreme concentration, where a person becomes oblivious to his or her surroundings while lost in thought. This can be achieved specifically by ambivalent stimulus coming from the female, whose biological purpose is to bind the male to her via a state of focused attention on her. Hormonal changes connected with sexual attraction make this focused state an extremely powerful motivator for the male.

Therefore, awareness of a woman's ambivalent, subcommunicated style of language is key to a modern man being able to enjoy lasting and happy relationships.

Being unaware of female subcommunication will tend to make a man weaker over time and will cause him many difficulties. When a man finds himself in this hypnotic state for extended periods of time, he is more likely to do almost anything to please his woman, even at the expense of his own welfare. The paradoxical result of this is that she will gradually lose her sexual and human interest in him. Eventually, she is likely to even feel *contempt* for him.

Consider courting. When courting, a man who puts a woman's daily welfare above his own may find that the successful courtship induces suspicion and jealousy in the woman. How is she to trust such a man, who could squander resources on a beguiling competitor, perhaps a younger woman!

Many pathological male reactions that can be observed within couple relationships are in fact a desperate defense mechanism, employed by men who have no skills with women. These reactions are meant to avoid the hypnotic state of focused attention on the female. For example:

- Violence used as an attempt to avoid the mental distress he suffers in connection with being faced with her subcommunication and ambivalence.
- Overt contempt of the woman and of women in general, used for the same purpose as above.

- Avoiding communication and attempts to isolate himself emotionally. Again, used for the same purposes.

Although a frustrated man may feel driven to employ such strategies as listed above, it should be fairly clear that those methods will prove to be ineffective in the long run.

An experienced man is able to make the best of this situation by relating to the woman in a challenging way, by indicating to her that he is aware of her subcommunication and that he understands it. A man is only able to challenge a woman in this way if he is aware of the hypnotic effect of female language and is able to deal with it properly. In absence of this skill he will:

- Either focus too much of his mental energy on her, and as a result become someone who is directed by her; Or
- Separate himself emotionally from her by cutting off communication with her.

Real-Life Experience

Franco once picked up a girl on the train with this line: "My name is Bond, James Bond." They met up and she seemed to be attracted but Franco noticed some signs of discomfort in her when he drew physically closer to her. Her reactive statement was: "You should shave your beard better", while touching his face. At first Franco believed this was a test but it was not so. Later on he understood that it was actually a *blueprint*. A blueprint is a subcommunicated emotion through which the woman is describing something that she likes or dislikes with all of her heart. Franco came to the conclusion — by free association — shave the beard → soft skin → woman's skin → *Bingo!* She likes women!

After a few weeks they became friends and the woman revealed the truth to Franco: she was completely lesbian and actually only would be with men in the role of a gold digger. She had been married four times and was always moving to a better apartment, paid for by men whom in reality she did not enjoy at all. She introduced Franco to her lesbian lover, too! So, it was all about her subcommunicated messages, which as you can see, revealed a great deal about her inner personality. Did any of her husbands understand this during their long marriages with her?

It should be noted that the ability to derive such definitive conclusions, as Franco did in the above example, is acquired by applying the lessons we are teaching you, repeatedly over time. The good news is, the moment you start to apply these lessons in your everyday interactions with women, the quicker you will deepen your understanding of Female Subcommunication. In other words, only with experience will you likely be able to make such snap judgments with accuracy. The above example *does not mean* that women preferring smoothly-shaven men are bisexual or lesbian. Franco's epiphany came from *understanding the subcommunication with this particular woman.*

She is Keeping her Options Open

Given the importance of subcommunication, let's dig in and find out more. As you will see, using subcommunication is a wonderful way of keeping one's options open, establishing plausible deniability while signaling intent, establishing boundaries, and for generally discussing any kind of topic without actually seeming to discuss it. While subcommunication infuriates men who haven't learned the language, make no mistake: women can and will exercise logic and direct speech, when it best suits their purpose!

Suppose you are out on a date with a woman, and you suggest a quick stop by your apartment to pick something up. Out of the blue she may say "OK, but we're not having sex." Most men would would be baffled by such a statement, especially if they had no previous intention of having sex anyway. However, what the woman is subcommunicating is something completely different than whether or not sex will actually occur.

Here is what's really happening: First, *she is testing your response.* If you get flustered by such a statement, she most certainly will not consider having sex with you. If your response is "Yeah, so, that was pretty random, who's talking about sex here?" the door for sexual engagement remains open.

Second, she is establishing a frame of interaction where she is taking no responsibility for the outcome. If she ends up naked in your bed, well, that's not her fault because she said "no sex." Never mind that it "just happened." Third, the next day she can tell anyone who asks "I specifically told him "no sex" before I went into his apartment."

Be that Man

Of course, anyone well-versed in the art of subcommunication understands all the nuances contained in such statements, but generally, these are not the people that will judge her behavior. We realize that many readers find this form of communication absolutely infuriating. Men have railed against it through the ages, complaining about women's deviousness and deceitfulness. What these men don't realize is that you can't have it both ways. You need to understand that for a woman to promote and maintain harmony within her environment, emotional states are more important to her than physical facts.

In other words, a woman may very well lie, or at least shade the truth, in order to preserve positive emotional states or prevent negative emotional states. Here is the most important part: even when women "lie" with their mouths, their bodies or emotions may be telling the real truth. The rare man that can penetrate these words and handle the truth — as the woman feels it — is a man who is very well-loved by women, indeed.

Women will never completely disclose their language to men, in part because women themselves dwell in this linguistic paradise mostly unconsciously. And they also do not disclose this language to us because they understand that a man truly versed in the art of subcommunication finds himself with great power over women. One key way for you to achieve this power is by cultivating the quality of *discretion*.

Cultivate Discretion

Discretion is the quality that we display as a signal to the woman that we are aware of the prevalence in society of the Madonna/whore Complex, and that we have personally dealt with it. You will read a great deal more about the Madonna/whore Complex in Chapters 16 and 17, but for now, realize that the Complex presents a real danger for a woman in our world. At the very least, the woman can sense danger from it in her subconscious mind. How do you subcommunicate to a woman that she is safe being sexual with you?

Men who are enjoying many sexual partners do not need to brag about their conquests as if they somehow "got lucky". Men who *want* to enjoy the company of many women must first learn to cultivate and display the quality of discretion. Such men are comfortable with women and their sexuality, and at the same time they know when to keep their mouths shut. They are not disturbed by female sexual expression and at the same time they know how to discreetly create the circumstances that will allow women the freedom to express themselves.

While he loves and enjoys sex and has no embarrassment about his sexual desires as a healthy man, sex is not something so rare and unusual for him that he is compelled to reveal private details to a woman's friends, or even his own friends.

Subcommunication in the Workplace

We believe that it is perfectly possible for men and women to be honest and direct with each other about their sexuality and emotional lives, but as long as subcommunication will be the female's preferred means of communication in this arena, we believe that men who live and work in our modern society should learn the art of subcommunication themselves. In social environments such as the workplace, this is particularly important.

Women can freely discuss dating and issues surrounding men in a mixed male/female work place using subcommunication. All women know that the term "hooking up" has several possible connotations, which may or may not mean sexual intercourse. Surprisingly, however, not that many men really understand this. On the contrary, men haven't had to develop the language of subcommunication and indirection, so men do not have the universal "code" that women seem to have regarding these topics.

The result on the modern, mixed workplace is often devastating. Women are free to talk and gossip, but men are not. The law in many jurisdictions states that language that makes a women merely *feel uncomfortable* in the workplace can constitute "sexual harassment", for which there are exceedingly stiff penalties. Basically, women today believe they have a legal right to feel good while they are at work. Strangely enough, they are right.

Men discussing women at work are usually applying male logic to situations that they have little experience with. This is, of course, a natural and normal thing for a man to do. Women recognize that males pooling their knowledge about individual women will very shortly develop a collective wit that will be applicable to *all* women. That is, these men will learn very quickly how to strip women of their power. For this reason, *some women* — although not all — may even *object strongly* to your acquisition of this knowledge.

Talk Like a Man

Men should always strive to cultivate the skills necessary to communicate in a manly way. Masculine subcommunication cannot be identical to feminine subcommunication, because that case the man will become too *effeminate*. The result of this will be that women will lose sexual attraction for him.

One of the aims of this book is to help you to actively improve the great mismatch between men and women when it comes to the art of communication and social intelligence. We believe that a man like you can acquire many of the skills that the average female now enjoys, without having to deny your own sexuality and masculine identity in order to do accomplish it.

John Gray, in his landmark book *Men are From Mars, Women are from Venus* [6], did a great job explaining how men and women communicate differently and how a man can effectively converse with a woman in the female language. What John Gray's book left out, however, was the crucial factor that a man must retain his masculinity in the relationship, and he cannot do so if he is engaging in too much feminine conversation with his partner over a long period of time. It is therefore vital to note that to be happy in your relationships with women, and in order to make them happy, you need to learn how to talk in the female language, and also to withdraw from that type of conversation at the appropriate time.

Practical Advice

You should seriously strive to cultivate a state of awareness when in the company of women, because female ambivalence and subcommunication are not things to be underestimated. In fact, if you allow yourself to relax too much and keep yourself in an unaware state, you will completely miss the meaning of female communication. Accept the fact that it is instinctual for women to express themselves in this indirect way.

To be able to deal with female subcommunication you need to shift from a mindset where you take everything she says at face value, to a mindset where you *interpret* what she says and put it through a subcommunication filter, as it were. Women do speak directly when it serves their purpose — some women more than others — and this must be accounted for as well. In fact, subcommunication is very effective when mixed with direct language. Also, remember that female subcommunication often has an underlying, *sexual meaning*! The more a woman subcommunicates in your presence, the more she may be sexually attracted to you.

In "politically-correct" countries it is common for many women — especially those not in touch with their femininity — to go through phases of dating a masculine man, followed by a nice, more effeminate man, to be followed by another masculine man, and so on. If you want to present a challenge to a modern woman, you have to learn how to keep yourself on the edge between masculine and feminine, but with an emphasis towards the masculine.

Therefore, to increase sexual and emotional arousal within a woman you will need to learn to shift between two identities in an almost schizophrenic manner. At times you will want to talk to women in a very masculine way: directly, succinctly and logically. At other times, you will want to talk to women in the same manner that a female friend might do. To be able to use subcommunication, you will need to continuously practice the art, because it is not the natural mode of conversation for a man.

Why you need to alternate between two styles of conversation? Because when it comes to the modern woman, she will alternate between preferring one style or the other, depending on the circumstances.

To make a woman happy — whether in the context of a committed relationship or in a lighter and less-committed interaction — you need to learn how to talk *womanese* while at the same time keeping your focus on your masculine attitude. If you leave out the art of speaking in womanese, you run the risk of becoming a cold, distant and boring person in her eyes. If you become too much of an expert in speaking womanese, she will no longer distinguish you from a woman and she will certainly lose attraction for you, whether quickly or over time.

The described alternation between male and female talk is actually extremely seductive to women. In seduction, anything which causes polarity will also be sexually stimulating. One basic aspect of the female psyche is the need for both stimulation and polarity. When you meet that need in a woman you make her happy. One of the main characteristics of today's woman is *boredom*, mixed with a search for emotional stimulation. By being the man who is able to talk womanese while at the same time remaining a real, masculine man, you put yourself far above almost all other men in her eyes. In fact, she will feel completely challenged when a man — who may even be a stereotypical computer programmer — will start to communicate with her in womanese while still leading her like a man.

An Example

David once worked as a contractor in the same office as a significantly younger woman — we'll call her "W" — who was also a contractor to the same client. That is, neither he nor she were employees. Now W was short — perhaps 5′3″ — and a bit thick — maybe 145 pounds — but with a definite sexual presence about her. She definitely worked what she had to her maximum advantage.

Some light banter and deep eye contact established mutual attraction early on. At one point, one of her supervisors — we'll call him "R" — entered the room in which they were working. The conversation turned abruptly from discussing "work" to this:

W: "Hey, R... such a jerk" (then playfully, to me) "He called me fat the other day."

R: "I did not!"

D: (playfully to her) "You're so huge."

W: "I'm not a pound over 300."

D: (playfully to her) "You're big as a barn. At least 400 pounds."

Now what the *hell* does her weight have to do with anything? This conversation is a total non-sequitur to the man not well-versed in subcommunication. But to the man fluent in womanese, this conversation is loaded with meaning. Specifically, she was acknowledging her attraction to David. And more importantly, this woman was indirectly, with subcommunication, evaluating *his* comfort level with *her* weight; whether or not David would judge her personally or make her feel bad in any way.

Note: W was not "subcommunicating" in a conscious way. She had simply learned through experience with men several lessons:

- Most men are judgemental about a woman's looks.
- Most men are more worried about what other men will think than they are about having a good time with a woman.
- Most men will "cop and blow," treating her with contempt after they get what they want from her.

Also through experience, W has learned how to swiftly and unconsciously evaluate men. It doesn't take much for a woman to figure out where a man stands with respect to her looks.

6 The Magic Pussy Syndrome

The power of the p-u-s-s-y — Best of Both Worlds, by Jay-Z and R. Kelly

MAGIC Pussy Syndrome (MPS) — a term coined by the authors — is the belief that because a woman has a pussy, she is entitled to special privileges at other people's expense. Such as: free drinks, free dinner, alimony, child support. The list goes on. In contrast, most guys we know pay for everything, and at retail prices.

Not all women suffer from this all the time. Most women have a bit of it in them, at least some of the time. For example, David Clare recently met a woman who said she had been dating two guys at the same time except that she wouldn't allow them to date other women. Now this was not an otherwise bad woman, in fact, she was a Good Girl. But she believed that because she was a woman, she had the right to behave this way, and that the men she dated did not.

In this chapter we will help you to quickly recognize the presence of MPS in the women that you encounter. We will explain the origins of this *mental disease* and provide you with powerful knowledge that will enable you to counteract it.

Recognizing MPS

As men we gain great power by *understanding* and *acknowledging* MPS, but at the same time, demonstrating that we refuse to take it seriously. This has the effect of short-circuiting the woman's aloofness and superior attitude. When a man shows that he is above a woman's MPS, she instinctively recognizes that she is dealing with a rare and superior male. In a healthy woman, this will wonderfully transform her into the pursuer of the man.

It can also be said that MPS serves as a screening mechanism for the woman. The majority of males will simply accept the MPS frame from her, while only the best males will recognize the frame but not accept it.

Your recognition of MPS can be a very effective method to eliminate women from your life who will prove to be a pain-in-the-ass, and you can accomplish this very early on in your interactions with them.

For example, suppose you have met an interesting and attractive woman. You arrange for a casual excursion, perhaps a visit to a new gallery opening, followed by a bite to eat afterwards. Really simple stuff. But she arrives late to the rendezvous (her excuse is irrelevant). Her next actions are critical: if she makes it up to you in some material way (like paying your ticket), you can safely let the lateness pass. If instead she follows her excuse with a request or a demand that you (or "we") do something that was not on the itinerary, and she expects you to pay for it, then you had better watch out! You should consider such behavior as a major red flag. If you don't check her behavior right then and there, she will worsen the behavior until she reaches your pain threshold. You will know you've reached that threshold by that shriveling feeling in your scrotum.[1]

If you let things get that far, what happens next will determine the entire course of any relationship you have with this woman. If you pitch a fit, you can now consider that she officially *owns* you. If *she* pitches a fit, and you supplicate in the hopes of calming her down, you are also officially owned. If you look deep into her eyes and tell her: "Hey, you know, it's been fun, but I gotta go" you may never hear from her again and wonder why.[2]

When you playfully tease a woman about her MPS, she will either withdraw from you, or she will transform herself into your

[1] JOSEPH I once dated a woman who had several boyfriends on the go at the same time. When she discovered that a former flame of mine had contacted me, she became infuriated. She felt it perfectly normal for her to maintain regular contact with past and present lovers, but completely unacceptable for me. She honestly believed this!

[2] FRANCO Finland, where I have been living now for many years, is an extremely feminist country. Most women are used to having the average guy totally figured out. These women will usually withdraw completely from the game when they meet a guy who keeps the frame "I, male, am the Prize", even if they are clearly attracted to such a man.

pursuer. Later in this chapter, we'll give some practical advice on how to properly handle a woman who displays clear signs of MPS. But for now, let's consider the motivations of the women whose MPS will cause them to retreat from a strong man who refuses to supplicate to them. In this group, let's discuss two sub-groups, the Low Self-Esteem (LSE) Group and the Political Group.

The LSE Group will naturally withdraw from interacting with a strong man, because they start to feel strong feelings of Low Self Esteem once they notice that the man is not promptly reacting as a supplicant to their MPS. Because these women are so accustomed to men supplicating, when they meet a man who simply *refuses* to do so, they take it as a personal insult. There is nothing you can do to correct such women, and unless you enjoy pain, it is best not to consider any serious relationship with them.

Any relationship started by such LSE women is a dead end in both directions. They will react with frustration to a man who does not supplicate to their MPS because they take it as a personal offense. On the other hand, they tend to become sexually frigid over time with men who *do* supplicate to their MPS, because the feminine part of their personality cannot derive lasting satisfaction out of such a dynamic.

The Political Group may withdraw from strong men for purely political reasons, *even if they are sexually attracted to the man in question.* This type of woman is very common at university campuses and within highly urban areas in the western world. These women are very often politically liberal, and they will often openly reject conventional notions of physical beauty.

Strangely enough, many women in these politically liberal environments, especially highly-educated university women, usually do not have much experience with masculine men at all. Many are prudes. And the men they *are* experienced with, are often a narrowly-defined group of men who self-identify as feminists. These male feminists also typically have little experience with women, and the experiences that they do have are generally reinforcing of their feminist viewpoints. You can often recognize the Political Group of MPS-sufferers by their perennial complaint: "There are no good men left!"[3]

Origins of MPS

Our hypothesis about the origin of the Magic Pussy Syndrome is that female sexual arousal is initiated especially by *words,* whereas male sexual arousal is initiated by *visual stimulation.* This creates an obvious mismatch between male and female sexuality, such that attractive women easily become overloaded with approaches from males. And males usually initiate interactions with women in such a way that leaves no doubt that they are basing their attraction solely on visual factors, which is usually not sufficient to arouse a woman or to convince a woman that continuing the interaction will be worth her while. The result of this is that, over time, many women come to believe that they are entitled to special advantages in our society. With men approaching and supplicating to women all the time, and demanding nothing more from the woman than that she look good, it becomes rather easy for women to exploit natural male sexuality in this way.

We believe that this mismatch between the male and female method of sexual approach may be created by nature with evolutionary purposes in mind. It is also possible to observe this type of mismatch in the animal species.

Please keep in mind that our observations here do not constitute value judgements against women. Women who suffer from the Magic Pussy Syndrome *are not bad women;* it's just how they are. Instead, consider this information as a value judgement for *your time.* If you easily get tranced-out by women, especially those wasting your time and money, learn how to deal with this *now,* before you find yourself deep into a relationship and thoroughly whipped.

[3]DAVID: The 26-year old, very attractive beautician who cuts my hair laughs at these prigs. According to her, there are good men everywhere.

Pussy Trance

The corresponding effect on men who haven't come to grips with the Magic Pussy Syndrome can be referred to as the *Pussy Trance*. The Pussy Trance is a generalization of the term "pussy whipped;" the difference is that being under the spell of a Pussy Trance happens to men that *aren't even in a sexual relationship with the woman*. These guys treat *all* women as if their pussies are magic. On the other hand, being pussy *whipped* implies that the man is in a relationship, where the woman is figuratively carrying his balls around in her purse.

Here are some indications that you may be in a Pussy Trance:

- If you find yourself in the company of a woman, doing something you don't really want to do, and you aren't sure how you came to be doing it, you're tranced.
- If you approach a woman you are interested in, and she ends up leading the discussion in directions that you don't want to go, you are tranced.
- If at any time, you make excuses for an adult woman's bad behavior just because she is a woman, you are either tranced or in danger of being tranced. If this bad behavior is affecting you adversely and you are still making excuses for the woman, you are definitely pussy tranced.

If you see yourself in any of the above situations, you are already ahead of most guys, merely by the fact that you are now taking steps to understand what's going on. Perhaps you have been unproductively spending a lot of time and money *dating*, with no romance developing. Break your trance now! Start by putting a value on yourself, your time and your money. When you are with a woman who starts to push against these values that you've set for yourself, give yourself a reality check. Ask yourself whether she is wasting your time and money, or whether the interaction or relationship is worthy of what you are putting into it.[4]

[4]DAVID I once went to lunch with a latin woman from South America. We

Practical Advice

You should recognize MPS as an integral psychological aspect of most women that needs to be taken into account when interacting with them or when seducing them. Biologically, *females choose for sex*. Therefore, let the woman feel as though she is has free reign to choose whether or not to have sex with you, without any pressure from you. If she feels the need for her ego to be stroked (i.e., she needs to feel as if her pussy is magic), it's no big deal. But never, ever allow a woman like this into a serious relationship with you, without first ensuring that everything else she brings to the table is complementary to or supportive of your non-sexual interests.

In other words, *let the woman choose for sex, but ensure that you, the man, are the one choosing her, the woman, for the relationship.* And you must absolutely ensure that your choice is not based on the fact she has a pussy and she happens to be physically attractive.

For you chivalrous fellows, be kind to elderly women, of course. An elderly woman who was raised with some manners will appreciate being treated like a lady.

When dealing with women who insist on being treated like ladies, first make sure that they are *acting* like ladies. If they aren't acting like ladies, don't treat them as if they are, no matter what they look like! If you do, you are definitely in a pussy trance, so stop it.

From our experience, the man that effectively neutralizes MPS can have open sexual relationships with multiple women simultaneously, without too much trouble. No woman in his harem will feel played when they have to make a conscious choice to engage on such a man's terms. Therefore, once you recognize MPS and deal with it properly, there no longer re-

ended up discussing politics somehow. She ended up practically *screaming* about George W. Bush, Iraq, baby killers, and so on. I tried to reason with her. Bad move! I had been tranced out with our delightful tete-a-tete and she tooled me hard. It's funny now to remember that I was thinking at the time that I didn't want to "take advantage" of her.

mains any need to lie to women about your desires or intentions.

7 Female Archetypes

Yup. She was a ho... fo' sho. — Andy, in "The 40 Year Old Virgin"

IN this chapter we classify women with broad strokes, picking out highlights and stereotypes of each kind of woman, and explaining the ramifications of each personality trait within a relationship. We also believe, from personal experience, that these terms "Good Girl", "Adventuress" and "Materialista" will be universally understood by all women of sufficient femininity to be attracted to normal, masculine men.

We categorize women into three simple classes, each with Sex Drive and Self-Esteem attributes. These labels were chosen for their common-sense utility. Here we offer distilled, common-sense advice on dealing with women based on our extensive, practical experience.

Many people hold the strong opinion that the only socially acceptable type of woman is the Good Girl, preferably with high self-esteem and a low sex drive. [1] Unfortunately, women publicly exhibiting any other behavior are judged rather harshly by our society.

In this chapter, we are going to teach you the basics about these Female Archetypes, and in the next chapter, we are going to get into greater detail on how to wisely choose the right women for your relationships.

*It is important to note that we make no value judgment against any woman whatsoever, either positively or negatively.*The terms "Good Girl," "Adventuress" and "Materialista" are simply useful labels, and all women will have elements of each type in greater or lesser degrees.

Our perspective is — in most cases, but not all — intended to supplement rather than supplant other author's experiences. For example, Robert Greene in *The Art of Seduction* [8] lists sixteen types of seduction "victims". The descriptive traits he ascribes to each type of victim are excellent characteristics to

---

[1] Bad behavin' women need good lovin' too!

bear in mind when you want to build rapport with someone. *Our* taxonomy deals on a more fundamental level, and allows for the calibration of *attraction* and *connection*. Our types and Greene's types can be viewed as *orthogonal*, and both his and ours can be used for great effect in seduction at any speed, and especially for relationship management, which we regard as simply long-term seduction.

The Adventuress

The Adventuress engages in sexual activity to gain emotional validation and public attention. For example, consider the shenanigans of Miss Paris Hilton, before she was incarcerated for violating probation. This attractive young woman is apparently *driven* to appear in public, even at the risk of making a spectacle of herself.

Other women of the Adventuress stripe in the popular view include Britney Spears, Angelina Jolie and Madonna.

The Materialista

The Materialista is a woman who actively trades sex or attention and affection for material "stuff." We use the term Materialista instead of "ho" or "golddigger" to indicate the general phenomenom of trading sex for stuff in general, versus trading sex directly for money, which is *prostitution*. Every woman has some Materialista in her. The behavior is natural, a result of evolutionary pressure.

Personally, we can't think of a better example of a Materialista than the brilliant and unique Zsa Zsa Gabor. Married nine (!) times, to a series of important and wealthy men, culminating in her latest and longest running marriage to Frédéric Prinz von Anhalt, a man recently described as an "aging German stud" in a late 2007 issue of *Vanity Fair* magazine. Interestingly enough,

Zsa Zsa's second husband, Conrad Hilton, was Paris Hilton's great-grandfather.

The Good Girl

The Good Girl is more *dissociative* between her sexual life and her presentation of herself to the outside world. In other words, she is more concerned about public appearances and not being viewed in a negative light with regards to her sexuality by her friends, family and society at large. In our experience, Good Girls are commonly interested in forming a close relationship with a man on the basis of love and mutual good feelings. As of the time of this writing, Jennifer Anniston — or at least her public persona that most people are familiar with — definitely qualifies as the USA's quintessential Good Girl.

Just as we do not make value judgements about Adventuresses and Materialistas, neither do we make value judgements about Good Girls. In fact, the label "Good Girl" refers primarily to how *society in general* judges her outward behavior. We believe that somewhere in the heart and mind of every Good Girl there is an Adventuress waiting to cut loose with the man of her dreams, and perhaps a Materialista who isn't adverse to at least the thought of "getting a good deal." And make no mistake, Good Girls can be just as ruthless pursuing their desires as any Adventuress or Materialista! The difference is in the underlying emotional motivations of each of these types of women.

Sex Drive and Self Esteem

The sex drive in humans is a powerful motivating force, in both men and women. Modern, western society downplays the female sex drive, while it both derides and exaggerates male sex drive. In truth, both males and females exhibit a wide range of sexual drive, which will also vary during different periods of an indivudual's life. The following terms "high drive" and "low drive" are not necessarily absolute, and in many cases should be qualified within the context of any existing relationship. One man's low-sex-drive woman may be another man's high-sex-drive woman.

Self Esteem is also a crucial factor in determining both the quality and tenor of adult relationships. Determining the woman's level of basic self esteem in conjunction with her level of sex drive — in advance of entering a romantic relationship — can save you a lot of time, money and heartache.

High Sex Drive

This category of woman is easily understood. It's important to realize that a woman's outward appearance, her morals, and her personality archetype has little direct bearing on whether or not she has a high sex drive, which we will denote by HD. Throughout this book, we will provide you with valuable information about how to detect the level of a woman's sex drive and how to augment it through your own words and actions. For now, it is vital to recognize that female sexuality is something beautiful and natural, and it should be appreciated and cherished, rather than feared or judged.

Low Sex Drive

Women with a lower sex drive (LD) will often place greater emphasis on the *raising* of children rather than on the *producing* of children. It is easy to see why nature has made it necessary to have both HD and LD women. We have found from experience, however, that LD women can sometimes be transformed into HD women, at least for a period of time. We will get into more detail in the following chapter, but for now consider that an LD woman who considers that she has her man all figured out will lose interest in him very fast. She will be more interested in a man who appears to be less preoccupied with sex and who is frequently away for long periods of time, especially with masculine-type missions and conquests.

High Self-Esteem

Women with high self-esteem (HSE) place heavy importance on safety for both themselves and their future offspring. When we say "safety", we are of course referring to physical safety. But we are also talking about emotional and *social* safety. [2] For almost any woman, her reputation and her standing among her peers is very important. However the HSE woman will be much less willing to accept bad behavior from you as something normal or tolerable. An HSE woman expects and demands the best for herself.

Low Self-Esteem

People with low self-esteem (LSE) will more frequently suffer from feelings of discouragement and a lack of self-worth. When they receive poor treatment, they are more likely to feel that it is justified and deserved. When they receive good treatment, they are more likely to discount such treatment as being undeserved and consider the donor of such treatment to be either misinformed or stupid. In the next chapter we will provide you with some simple and elegant tests that will help you to detect the level of self-esteem in women.

Two Modern Archetypes

The following paragraphs describe two types of women common in the urban west, especially in the cosmopolitan core of large cities.

The Situational Ten

The most attractive woman within a social circle or a subculture dominated by males is a *Situational* Ten. She is the woman who most all of the men in the circle desire, and *she knows it*.

[2] Social Safety is one of the most important considerations for a woman thinking about starting a sexual relationship with a man.

In some cases, such women may not be looked at twice in a nightclub or anywhere outside of her situational circumstance. But due to their intellect or athletic ability, or some other capability to enjoy relatively-masculine endeavors, these women are able to achieve material success in male-dominated fields. These women are highly status conscious, in many cases choosing such fields with full knowledge they will have the the "pick of the litter" when it comes to men. Courting or seducing these women is hard because it is absolutely impossible to fake status in these fields; achievement is public knowledge.

Any given nightclub, sporting event, or social activity will also have its Situational Ten. However, in these cases, the Situational Ten is highly likely to be "hot" in the popular culture sense as well.

The Eternally Single Woman

Many modern, liberated women, beneficiaries of the pioneering work of early feminists, have reached material and physical security undreamed of by previous generations. Some of this progress has occurred due to gender-based affirmative action. Women of the current generation are encouraged to postpone marriage and children, to travel and see the world. These physical and emotional explorations allow women to develop sexual and emotional sophistication previously unheard of. The result of this is that the modern woman suffers from rising expectations even as she moves through repeated failures of successive relationships. We call such a woman the Eternally Single Woman (ESW).

By the time a modern, urban, well-educated, well-read, well-traveled woman reaches her mid-30s, she has most likely experienced a much wider variety of sexual experience than 90% of the males her age. This presents her with a problem: given that she is physically secure and financially self-sufficient, her need for a man revolves around satisfying only her sexual and emotional needs. Compounding this problem is that her expectations rise with each successive relationship, while her value for bearing children simultaneously declines.

The ESW is a creature of the modern, urban west. She typically has a college education. She may consider herself well-traveled, having taken trips to exotic locations and stayed in luxurious hotels. She may consider herself well-read; a consumer of best-sellers. She may have a lucrative job, which she considers as her career. And yet she may be petrified at work when she is finally required to be responsible for the bottom line.

The ESW most likely has a cloud of men willing — if not eager — to invest their time with her, in exchange for very little return to themselves. She does not treat these men with respect, but when she needs something distasteful done, she can always find a man to perform the task. She is, unfortunately, not sexually attracted to these men. In the best case, she may feel sorry for these guys, but she will not have sex with them. Why should she, when they will do her work for free?

As you may imagine, these women often lead very frustrating lives. While on the one hand they enjoy material success and the adoration of men, on the other hand they find themselves moving about freely in a world with so few "real" men. Women, just like men, are constantly being fed mixed messages about what it means to be a "real" man or a "real" woman. There is an endless stream of men willing and able to buy them dinners, take them on vacations, or lend a sympathetic ear when times are rough, but hardly *any* men available to them that they find sexually appealing. Women long for an emotionally strong man to lead and protect them, and instead they find themselves surrounded by "male girlfriends"; guys that are sweet, kind and understanding, but who have the same sex(less!) appeal as any one of their girlfriends.

Practical Advice

Most men today are still raised with old-fashioned values based on chivalry. Many men haven't a clue just how much sexual experience women have had. Their wives and girlfriends aren't going to tell them either, lest they get tarred with a label of "slut" or "whore." Your review of this chapter on common female archetypes should give you a new perspective on women and expand your horizons as to what is possible in the realm of male-female relationships. Please pay particularly close attention to the next chapter, where we will delve more deeply into the Female Archetypes and how to choose wisely for your relationships.

8 Screening for the Archetypes

It is a truth universally acknowledged, that a single man in possession of a good fortune, must be in want of a wife.
— the brilliant *Pride and Prejudice*, by Jane Austen.

IN Chapter 7 on Female Archetypes, we touched briefly on the distinction that can be made between an Adventuress, a Materialista and a Good Girl. These distinctions are based on emotional responses and behavior, and not by things like a woman's physical looks or her manner of dressing. Furthermore, these distinctions are most useful during interactions which have an element of *high polarity*. That is, the more feminine the woman's behavior, the easier it is for you to understand her motivations and observe how she reacts emotionally. Women with more masculine character traits tend to suppress their emotional expression, which reduces the effectiveness of these categories.

The goal of this chapter is to delve further into the Archetypes, and to assist you in identifying particular types of women when you encounter them. Most men enter relationships with the opposite sex *blindly*, mistaking sexual chemistry for long-term compatibility. The purpose of *screening* is to help you to rationally observe the principal types of women that exist in the world, so that you can make wise choices regarding your time, energy, and *emotions*, *before* you get sexually involved with anyone.

Why is screening so important? Sexual intercourse produces a flood of chemicals in the bloodstream which, by nature, make it much more difficult for most people to extract themselves from the relationship after the fact. On the positive side, as a practical man you want to spend your time, energy and money wisely in life. Spending part of your life on a woman who turns out to be totally incompatible with your goals and lifestyle is tantamount to *stealing* that time, from both yourself and from the women who *are* worthy of you. Therefore, screening is a vital tool in your arsenal as a happy, successful modern man.

If we have any mantra, it's this: love the woman for who and what she really is, not for who you wish her to be, or for who society says she should be. This single piece of advice, coupled with the skills for recognizing types of women, will revolutionize your skill in relationships with women.

The Good Girl

One Good Woman. What every man needs. In our model of the female archetypes, the Good Girl derives emotional satisfaction from being perceived as following socially-prescribed norms, especially those associated with sexual behavior. In short, Good Girls generally aren't promiscuous, and prefer to limit sexual involvement to more loving and committed relationships. Even still, however, not all Good Girls are suitable for long term, loving relationships.

Remember that the archetype label "Good Girl" is not to be confused with making a moral judgment about a woman. A woman in a search for a committed, monogamous relationship with a man can be just as ruthless as any other woman in going after what she wants. If you are a man of high value, she may very well try to mold her personality to conform to what she believes you are looking for in a woman, in order to secure a relationship with you[1]. This can even include outright dishonesty. Therefore it is inadvisable to consider a serious, long-term relationship with *any* woman until you have the wisdom that comes with experience and you are an expert at the screening process.

The HSE Case

A Good Girl with healthy self-esteem (HSE) makes appropriate long-term relationship material for *most* men, especially when sex drives are well-matched. This latter point is crucial; An HD woman paired with a low or much lower-drive man is liable to get very cranky and restless. A woman with a low or much-lower sex drive may well use sex to manipulate the man in

[1]as in the bait-and-switch game, which we discuss in a following chapter

the relationship. A Good Girl who is not satisfied sexually, or conversely, one who feels sexually pressured, is likely to get feelings of depression and anxiety due to such a mismatch in sexual drives.

Look for the following points when screening for a Good Girl with high self-esteem:

- She tends to place value on all her relationships, whether with her family, friends, and mates.
- She is in touch with her feminine sexuality and her sexual desire. She may love sex as much as any other woman, but she prefers it with a man whom she is in a committed relationship with.
- She is able to accept you as a man who is also a sexual human being.
- She respects the masculine world without trying to be a man herself or act like a man.
- She is comfortable in a wide range of social situations.
- She will not tolerate much abuse of any kind from anyone, whether friends, family or mates.

The LSE Case

A Good Girl with low self-esteem (LSE) may be as ruthless as any other kind of woman, and even more dangerous, as she cloaks her ambition under what is otherwise socially-acceptable behavior. With a woman having a high libido (HD), there will be lots drama. Low-libido women (LD) will often use sex within a relationship to manipulate her man, and quite often to his material disadvantage.

Low-self esteem Good Girls are not that hard to recognize. This woman will be the one hissing at an edgy scene in a movie. She will be uncomfortable in a wide range of social situations, preferring to spend her time in social situations with very little risk. She will correct her man, in public, when her opinion of his actions violate what she perceives as socially acceptable. She will also tolerate fairly emotionally abusive situations as long as such are perceived by her to be more socially acceptable than the alternative. For example, consider how the divorce rate has risen to staggering levels once the stigma of divorce was removed through the legal expedient of "no-fault divorce."[2]

The Adventuress

As mentioned in the previous chapter, these women are primarily motivated by both sexual gratification and male attention. They are excellent candidates for women to have casual and/or short-term relationships with.

However, men with sensitive hearts need to be particularly careful with this type of woman. It is a commonly-held myth in our society that men are universally able to have random sex with women without suffering any emotional attachment, and that *all* women *require* a deep emotional connection before being able to enjoy sex with a man. In the face of real-life experience with Adventuresses, this myth unravels in a swift and shocking way for many men.

Adventuresses typically get bored with monogamy very easily. Remember, they are motivated primarily by sexual excitement and male validation. Therefore, supplicating to such a woman, or trying to get her settled down into a monogamous relationship, or wishing for her to change her promiscuous ways, is a sure recipe for heartbreak. When a woman talks a lot about how much she values her freedom and not being tied down, pay very close attention!

If you are ready for a casual, no-strings-attached relationship, however, these women can often be ideal. The proper way to interact with such a woman is *always* in a non-judgmental, non-

[2]While the actual percentage is unclear, statistical studies repeatedly show that women initiate divorce much more often than men, ranging from 65 to 91% of cases, depending on the source.

jealous fashion.

You can recognize an Adventuress by observing her dating patterns. An Adventuress who is young or inexperienced may have a trail of broken-hearted men behind her. She will generally be more open to discussing sexual topics. Dating and courtship will cause her to get bored quickly, while proper physical escalation will excite her. You will more readily discern the difference as you gain experience.

It should be noted that Adventuresses can often have many Good Girl qualities, especially when it comes to their *platonic* relationships. Just be very careful that you do not confuse a woman's kindness and friendliness with sexual loyalty and devotion.

The HSE Case

A woman who is an HSE Adventuress is a woman who loves pleasure for it's own sake. She is not bound by typical social conventions when it come to her sexuality. Therefore, an HSE Adventuress is a woman who thrives on male attention and/or sexual variety, but she is not doing so in a self-destructive way. A list of well-known HSE Adventuresses would include the likes of Madonna and Angelina Jolie, although both of these women have slowed down considerably in the last few years or so.

The LSE Case

The Adventuress is often typified by self-destructive behavior, therefore many Adventuress you will meet will be of the LSE variety. An LSE Adventuress may very well sabotage a perfectly good relationship with you, by cheating for example, because an LSE woman simply cannot accept that she *deserves* a stable, monogamous relationship with a good man. If you attempt to impose one on her she is likely to rebel. As already mentioned, an Adventuress also craves *sexual variety* and an LSE woman will jeopardize her health, her other relationships, and sometimes her physical and mental safety in order to satisfy her emotional or physical cravings.

The Materialista

Materialistas are primarily motivated by material wealth, by money, prestige and the power that such things bring. An inexperienced, tactless Materialista may easily get upset at the suggestion that you split the bill on dates, whereas a more sophisticated Materialista may actually bait you by offering to pay on occasion, knowing that you will be compelled to pay later when it *really* counts.[3]

You will easily recognize such women by their conversation. Is she primarily interested in talking about money and the things money can buy? A favorite verbal technique of women is to present things to you in the third person, such as "My girlfriend is *so lucky*; her boyfriend just flew her to Vegas first class, and they are staying in the presidential suite and..."

If you find that a woman's level of affection towards you rises and falls consistently with the amount of money you are spending on her, then you can bet you have a Materialista on your hands.

It is important to bear in mind that women with traits of a Materialista are first and foremost human animals in as much need of love and affection as any Good Girl who is determined to preserve her chastity. But loving a Materialista as if she were a Good Girl is a recipe for disaster. If she's a Materialista, and you love her, love her on *her* terms as a Materialista, not on *your* terms as if she was a Good Girl. If you must have a Good Girl, go find one.

We are confident in saying that virtually all women have a bit of Materialista in them. Throughout the ages, female survival depended on the skills of getting men into a position where they would provide in a material way for the women, and do so willingly. There is therefore no point in expressing anger or frustration when a woman demands that you pay for her drinks or food. Just realize that some women are more bent on extracting wealth from men than others. It is up to you as

[3] A Good Girl may also get upset, but for a different reason: the man picking up the tab is the socially-approved manner of courtship.

a Modern Man to determine what *your* standards are, which women will enjoy a place in your life and on what terms.

The key to handling a Materialista, or handling any women showing a bit of materialism in her behavior is to "pimp" her. That is, you must put the woman to work for you, by having her do little things for your benefit, at your convenience, at her expense. This might be cooking or cleaning for you, or running errands to the market, or ordering items from the internet. Real-life prostitutes require a full-time, professional pimp, who handles the business side of her operations, and provides emotional support when necessary. The rest of us need only to recognize the symptoms of the Materialista when they emerge, and take immediate steps to deal with them.

Again, a certain amount of Materialista behavior is natural and normal in any healthy woman, because any normal girl wants to get the best deal that she can. We choose to celebrate this fact and turn the woman's nature to our advantage. Even better, when in a committed relationship with such a woman, this behavior can be turned to mutual advantage, benefitting the relationship as a whole.

The bottom line is, *she needs to be working for you*; not the other way around. You need to set and maintain a strong frame of you and her against the world rather than you and her against each other. This means you must be a man who knows how to lead a woman and cannot be intimidated — either by her or by other men.[4]

[4]Joseph: One night while out at a swanky place a female friend pointed out a well-dressed, much older man and said "He wants to buy me a drink Joseph! What should I do?" I said to tell him that you will gladly accept a drink, for yourself and your friend (me). This man bought us three drinks each before we all went our separate ways, with her and I heading back to my place. My friend gave the man companionship in exchange for the free drinks, and he left happy. She saved her more romantic affections for *me*. It worked well for me because of my non-judgmental, non jealous attitude, and my *encouragement* of the friendly exchange that took place.

The HSE Case

HSE Materialistas can be dangerous — to your wallet, your pride, and your emotions — and conversely they can be a lot of fun if you know what you are doing. In this case, you will need great inner strength. If you have any tendency to buy a woman's favor through gifts, a Materialista is not for you. However, if you are steadfast in your principles and refuse to pay for the affections of women, *and* if you are completely non-jealous and happy for her to get her material needs met elsewhere, such a woman can learn to appreciate a modern man very much. Materialistas need love too, and if she has a High Sex Drive (HD), she will find you very appealing indeed, if you embody the above-mentioned qualities.

It needs to be mentioned that a Low Sex Drive (LD) Materialistas can be *particularly dangerous* for a man. These women *understand* the male sexual drive, yet they do not share the same passion for sex. Since they are very calculating and always angling for money, they are able to *fake* sexual arousal fairly adeptly. They can also withdraw sexual affection quite easily, and they do! It is a trap designed to make the man spend more money in order to revive what he mistakenly experienced as passion coming from the woman.

The LSE Case

Even though Materialistas are primarily motivated by money, a woman who is also LSE will be ineffective. An LSE woman has trouble accepting anything of true value from anyone. An LSE Materialista will also be virtually impossible to satisfy, because not only does she require more and more material treatment, as all Materialistas do, but she also will get less and less satisfaction from such treatment because of her LSE. In addition, she will "price herself" very low. Streetwalkers are very much in this category, having nothing other than sex to offer any man besides her pimp, to whom she offers money in exchange for emotional support.

Practical Advice

Remember, *these categories are generalized guidelines implying no value judgement on any woman.* We believe these female responses are evolutionarily derived and that they can be overridden or otherwise suppressed by most healthy women.

Also keep in mind that no woman is one hundred per cent Good Girl, Adventuress or Materialista. People are usually a combination of complex traits. But these stereotypes can prove to be an excellent guide for you when you are making your dating choices.

Our goal with this book is to help you love women for who they truly are, and not for who you might wish for them to be. Once you can accept the fact that women often come with very different motivations when it comes to male-female relationships, *only then* will you be in a position to confidently pick and choose which women will be allowed space in your life, and in what capacity.

Are you looking for a series of exciting, short-term relationships with women? Then, as long as you are sure you can tolerate a woman's wilder side, you'll want to focus your energy on Adventuresses. Do you want to be a Gigolo? Then, ideally, Materialistas who have at least some sense of loyalty and principle will be your targets. Are you ready to settle down and start a nuclear family with children? Then the Good Girl is the type of woman you will want to devote your time and energy to.

Above all, use this information as data-gathering for mere facts. *Do not impose moral judgments upon women or get upset that they behave the way that they do.* This is merely nature at work and also part of the effects of our modern, western culture. If you find you are having difficulty accepting women as they fall under these various categories, please review the chapter on the Madonna/whore Complex very carefully.

Next, we will drill down into the psychological dynamics of women with varying levels of self-esteem. We will discuss the different styles of interactions that you can expect with such women, and help you to recognize their archetypes *before* you commit yourself to a relationship.

9 Female Self Esteem

Every day I fight a war against a mirror
I can't take the person staring back at me
I'm a hazard to myself
don't let me get me
I'm my own worst enemy
— *Hazard to Myself* by Pink

FEMALE self-esteem is a poorly understood subject for most men. To properly understand this part of our book it is important to get acquainted with a concept known as "basic trust." This concept was described first by Milton H. Erickson, and it means that every person has a more or less of a basic sense of trust, including the ability to depend on oneself as well as on others. Read this chapter carefully, because this concept will have a tremendous impact on the quality and outcome of your relationships with women. It is crucial to detect — very early on — the level of basic trust of any woman that you meet, in order for you to decide which direction to take with her.

In this book, we divide women into two groups in regards to their self-esteem:

- HSE: women with high self-esteem
- LSE: women with low self-esteem

Being able to detect a woman's own notion of her self-esteem provides you with crucial information about how she feels about herself and how she views the world around her.

As a rule of thumb, the HSE woman has a high degree of basic trust. She will have a basic internal certainty that she is good, worthy and fit as a woman, and she will have a healthy confidence in her ability to depend on both herself and other people.

On the other hand, the LSE woman has a low degree of basic trust. She may view herself as worthless, bad, and/or not useful to herself or anyone else. Unfortunately, many LSE women believe that they deserve to be abused by men, and may in fact consciously or unconsciously goad men into abusive acts against them, which only serve to reinforce their self-image.

It is important to note that our division between HSE and LSE describes end-member behavior along a spectrum. Most women have both HSE and LSE characteristics, and can display either or both, depending on the context of interaction that they find themselves in.

Basic Trust

There is some determinism in this feature. Modern academic psychology has — at least in the media — overrated the potential that psycho-therapeutic techniques have to improve a person's self-esteem. What happens in reality is that if you detect LSE in a woman, she may have that feature for a long, long time, and in many cases, forever.

It is important to make wise choices with your time and energy. While some people may label you as callous and uncaring for refusing to get into relationships with LSE women, it is the course of wisdom to realize that many unpleasant features of such relationships will be rather permanent, in spite of your best efforts to help such a woman or to show her understanding and compassion.

The Early Frame Announcement

Detecting a woman's self-esteem is strictly linked with a concept we have coined as the Early Frame Announcement (EFA). As a rule, a woman will say or do something early on in a relationship, by which she will unwittingly reveal the degree of her self-esteem and also what she expects from her relationships with men. Therefore, it is important that you pay very close attention to what a woman does and says at the very beginning of any relationship. Never forget that detecting the level of her self-esteem is crucial for you to know where to go and where not to go in your dealings with her.

It is also very important to understand well the concept of *frame* when dealing with women, or any other type of human relationship for that matter. A frame is a psychological environment which defines interactions and contexts. For example:

- "Doctors are good people who help others" is one frame
- "Doctors are sadistic people who enjoy seeing blood" is a different frame.

Maybe doctors are both good *and* sadistic, or perhaps they are neither. The frames used when talking about such a topic are not to be confused with absolute truth on a matter; they only reveal details about someone's subjective experience. Therefore, a frame is very often connected with one's subjective experience. In fact, "basic trust" is also a frame which is highly subjective. People with high self-esteem might dwell on an idea that a terrorist may drop an atomic bomb on some town tomorrow or the next day. However, whether or not that happens in reality is another matter.

Relationship with Sexuality

If read correctly, the woman's EFA will determine the course of her behavior in your relationship together, with mathematical precision. One of the most important features of an LSE woman is her inability to receive or appreciate good things. A woman with LSE may relate to her sexuality as something bad, dangerous, painful and/or sad. On the other hand, a woman with HSE will usually relate to her sexuality as something joyful, beautiful, interesting and/or positive.

Take for example an EFA delivered via a statement such as, "I don't like to receive compliments." Such a comment from a woman, given early on in your interaction with her, should cause LSE alarm bells to start ringing in your head. It is very important that you never lose sight of the fact that women are extremely serious about their EFAs. What this woman is quite clearly subcommuniating — very early on — is: "I feel that I do not deserve good things from you or from anyone else."

Such a lack of basic trust will have the tendency to *escalate* in a relationship. It may start with a frame of "I do not like compliments." Later on in the relationship a woman like this will typically make statements like, "I do not feel comfortable with you. I feel you may become violent" or, "I think you are a pig when you want sex" or, "you do not understand my depression", and so on.

An important feature of the LSE woman is to introduce the topic of sexuality early on in the relationship, while at the same time being dissociative in regards to it. "Dissociative" means that there is not a strong, conscious connection between her mind and her body. For example, she may say something on the very first meeting such as, "I like strong men who can make me scream," but then refuse to have sex afterwards.

Another important, core feature of the LSE woman is a deep need for figuratively castrating men *psychologically*. In fact, their basic low level of self-esteem makes them see the world from a position of *envy*. On the other hand, an HSE woman views the world from a position of *gratitude*.

Let us now take a brief look at some of the internal belief systems of both HSE and LSE women.

Internal Beliefs of the HSE woman

- "I am good. I am worthy."
- "I deserve all the good things that I can get."
- "I am willing to give good things to other people and I know that I will still have enough for myself."
- "Sexuality is a joyful thing."
- "Men love me."
- "I love men."

Internal Beliefs of the LSE woman

- "I am bad. I am worthless."
- "I do not deserve good things from others."
- "I feel I cannot give anything positive to anyone, not even to myself."
- "Sex is dirty, nasty, destructive."
- "Men hate me."
- "I hate/am afraid of men."

How LSE and HSE Women Test Men Differently

Every woman has a basic need to test the potential and strength of a man early on in an interaction, as well as *throughout* the duration of any relationship with him. This holds true for interactions which the woman intends as short-term, and even more so if she has a longer-term relationship or marriage in mind.

As we've already discussed, you can detect whether a woman is LSE or HSE by her EFA. You can also detect whether she is LSE or HSE from the way she tests you, especially early on. By default, an HSE woman's tests are designed to test your self-worth. An LSE woman's tests are directed to test how destructive you can be. A woman tests you based on her view of the world. And her view of the world is determined by the level of her basic trust.

For example, when a woman says something like, "My last boyfriend was beating me all the time," this is quite clearly an LSE type of test. On the other hand, if she says something like, "I just love guys who interrupt me when I talk", with a hint of sarcasm, after you've made the mistake of interrupting her, that would be an HSE test.

Therefore, if the woman says, "My boyfriend was beating me all the time," she is testing you to see if either a) You are going to take part in her misery and become her therapist (if you choose this route, we guarantee that *you will not be enjoying a sexual relationship with this woman.*); or b) whether you are going to beat her in the same way that her former boyfriend did, in which case, the sex could be really hot.

From the LSE woman's point of view you have "value" for her only if you do one of the above two things. If you try to give her genuinely good things, she will simply not believe that this is possible. She will consider you to be either weak or a liar.

On the other hand, an HSE woman, by calling you on interrupting her, is testing for whether you are dependent on her judgment of you for your own self esteem. If you freak out or get defensive, you are done.

She is also testing you to see whether you are intelligent enough to understand that she values how she feels and what she says. You can keep interrupting her of course; but that's not really the issue at hand. The core purpose of her test is in fact to detect whether your level of self-esteem is at her level or above. In this way she can decide whether or not you are a man that she can *feel safe* with.

Awareness of Her Own Sexuality

A woman's awareness of her own sexuality is critically important. Imagine for a moment that a woman's sexual, instinctual world is like the motor of a car, and her *awareness* of that instinctual world is like the steering wheel.

An LSE woman is usually in poor touch with her "motor", such that she may be under the influence of very strong sexual instincts and/or poor sexual instincts, but in either case, her awareness (driving skills) of those instincts will be quite poor. It is similar to a situation where a person is driving a more or less powerful Ferrari, but the driver doesn't have very much skill or experience with regards to driving that type of car.

On the other hand, you can recognize an HSE woman because of her skillful touch on the 'steering wheel'. She knows where she is going and what she is doing, whether her "motor" (sex drive) is very powerful or not.

The relationship of the LSE woman with her body is poor and for this reason she tends to be very dissociative. On the other hand, an HSE woman is not so dissociative. It should be noted, however, that dissociation is an element which is always present, to one degree or another, in *all* female sexuality.

LSE/HSE Male-Female Tests

You can also screen a woman for her LSE/HSE features by observing what arouses her in the course of a seduction.We call these LSE/HSE Male-Female Tests. These are simple tests you can run on a woman to detect the level of her self-esteem, early on.

The LSE Threshold Test

We would never advocate doing this if it would not be for your safety. For the sake of your safety is very important that you know early on whether a woman is LSE or not. Please do not try this at home with your long-term partner! This is a test to be run early on in a relationship, to lest for a woman's level of self esteem, *before* you find yourself deep into a long-term relationship with her.

When you meet a woman, as an early test, you can say or do something that is slightly-lowering to her self-esteem. For example, this could be giving her an order in a slightly harsher way than normal, or by making fun of her and then escalating such teasing. By doing this, you will find the level which we refer to as her *Self-Esteem (SE) Threshold.*

The LSE Threshold is a reaction that a woman will present when you run this test on her. An HSE woman, for example, will react at a certain point with a statement like, "This is unacceptable! You don't do this to me!" From this point, you can measure the degree of her self-esteem in a certain way. On the other hand, if you escalate with harsher treatment on a woman with bad LSE, you will be able to go much further without her defending herself in an effective manner. Some LSE women will be able to tolerate very harsh treatment without presenting the SE Threshold.

A woman will stop you once you reach her threshold. If the woman is HSE and you like her, then it should be obvious that you'll want to end the test at this point. Simply acknowledge her objection and change the subject.

Eliciting Values about her Former Relationships

"Eliciting Values" means to find out about the particular abstract beliefs that a woman has, which in turn produce the feelings that are important to her in a relationship. You cannot do this in a direct way, otherwise you will give her the impression that you are too much of a nice guy and hence lower her attraction for you. For example, you would never, ever want to ask something direct like, "am I your type?"; rather, you have to elicit this information in an indirect way.

Indirect simply means that you are finding out about her values without her noticing that you are doing so. This can be done by using active listening skills. Having active listening skills means that you put aside your own values for the moment, and you relax and listen carefully to what she says about her past relationships. If she stops or changes subject you can kindly redirect her with phrases such as:

- "And?"
- "Oh that sounds interesting! I can't believe it really happened..."
- "Amazing story! How did that happen?"

You absolutely must elicit a woman's values in regards to one extremely-important thing, and that is, how she reacts to abuse.

Remember this: how a woman reacts to abuse is crucial information that will help you to determine where she is on the LSE/HSE spectrum. Therefore, when you find out the history of her former relationships, what you especially need to look for is, 'has she been psychologically and/or physically abused, in a repetitive fashion, by her former male partners?' If she has been in that scenario very often, then you can be very sure that she is LSE. While there is absolutely no excuse for continuing to beat on another human being, adults also have the responsibility to immediately and permanently remove themselves from unacceptable situations.

Presenting Yourself as Free-Minded

This is a technique to have her open up to you, so that she tells you what you really want to know. It is also a good test for HSE/LSE.

There is a secret agreement amongst women; they talk in a completely free-minded way about everything amongst themselves. This free-minded conversation that women have comes across as *subcommunication* when translated into the male language. Women keep this facet of their conversations with other women a secret from men, and they sometimes do this consciously and sometimes unconsciously.

The key here is, when you first approach a woman, you should let her know in a subtle way that you are a free-minded individual. As an example, you could say something like:

- "I can't believe how those guys made such a big deal about the mayor's affair. They are all adults after all."
- "I think it is so stupid when people make such a fuss about sexual minorities!"
- "I can understand that women who are frustrated in their marriage sometimes will end up seeking out a more adult, satisfying love."

Sooner or later, sincere comments like this from you will invariably cause any woman to open up. She will start to tell you things she would never imagine discussing with her husband or boyfriend, but only with her girlfriends.

But be careful: don't do this from the frame of the nice guy, who is trying to make up for his own lack of attractive qualities by presenting himself as the overly-sympathetic listener who has nothing better to do than agree with everything that comes out of the woman's mouth. By doing that, you will ruin the sexual attraction. Your goal here is not to become another one of her girlfriends. Instead, be sure to put some tension and excitement into the conversation; disagree with her on occasion and tease her a bit at other times.

Testing her Level of Self-Esteem

Once a woman is comfortable with you and convinced that you are a free-minded person, she will start to open up to you about everything; what she likes, her sexuality, her former relationships and so on. Once you know what you want to know, you can then test her by becoming a little bit nastier and wilder in your free-mindedness. In other words, become progressively more crude. If she is LSE, she will giggle and become even more attracted to you. This is because the LSE woman has very chaotic and non-defined borders of the Ego, and they easily let strangers into their sphere of personal intimacy.

On the other hand, an HSE woman will do something to try to stop you, because she will begin to feel some uneasiness. Caution: this does not mean that the HSE woman is not free-minded. Instead, this usually means that her self-esteem reacts to your attack on her core values by defending the borders of her intimacy.

The less a woman defends an attack against her personal, intimate boundaries, the more she is LSE. The more a woman defends against such an attack, the more she is HSE, with one important exception: the LSE LD women.

The Low Self-Esteem (LSE), Low Sex-Drive (LD) woman may *seem* to be defending the borders of her intimacy while you are becoming more crude in your speech, but she is usually doing this out of *a fear of sexual intimacy*. Such a woman lacks the capacity to really enjoy sex, and this is *not* due to a healthy level of self-esteem on her part. Therefore, it is important to know about and recognize this sub-group of women.

After you have performed this basic test of the woman's free-mindedness, you then must determine whether there are elements of self-destructiveness in her.

The Tendency towards Self-Destructiveness

Once you gain experience with testing women for HSE/LSE, you will begin to notice that the HSE woman has a lot of mental space between the physical and the psychological part of her sexuality. In other words, she behaves like a person who is constantly testing your personality, and she will take the time to do so without rushing into any kind of sexual action with you. The HSE woman can do this because of her superior awareness of her own sexuality.

On the other hand, an LSE woman will seem to be in a big rush — once you elicit her sexuality with your seductive skills — in either one of two directions. In one direction, she may be in a hurry to deny her own sexuality, by making comments like "I am not that kind of a woman!" This is a distinctive trait of the LSE LD woman.

Alternatively, she may be in a relative hurry to grab your male sexual organ and to jump all over you. This is a distinctive trait of the LSE HD woman. The women of this sub-group may introduce sexual elements early on in your interaction, even before any overt approach coming from you.

HSE women may also have sex with you quite quickly, but you will notice that before an HSE woman does so, she will take the time to more carefully test your personality. Not testing your personality prior to having sex is almost invariably a sign of LSE.

Another important feature of the HSE woman is that she will always test you for *safety*. For a healthy women, she is concerned with three primary aspects of safety: physical, psychological, and *social* safety.

This will not be an easy one to detect; women with LSE can *also* test you for safety, but they will do so from a completely different perspective than HSE women. LSE women will test you for safety from a position of *fear*. LSE women who have deep damage to their self-esteem will also test you for *abuse*. It is very sad to say, but some LSE women will consider a man as a high-value prospect if he demonstrates the capability for abusing them.

On the other hand, when an HSE woman tests you for safety, what she is after is the feeling that she can safely be with you as an emotional and sexual human being. She is also concerned with her reputation in the community and among her friends and family. This is deeply programmed into a woman on the biological level. An HSE woman understands well about the chance for pregnancy and of the necessity of wisely choosing a suitable partner before she engages in the act of sex.

When an HSE woman tests you for safety, she will often seem to be acting in quite a selfish manner from your perspective as a man and that is certainly the case. However, the HSE woman's selfishness will not have destructive elements within it. Rather, there will be always be an aspect of looking out for her own emotional, physical and social well being.

Practical Advice

Why, therefore, should you always test a woman for her level of self-esteem? Because amongst all of the discernible traits of her personality, her self-esteem is one factor that will definitively influence the course of your interaction with her. This holds true whether the interaction be will be short-term, long-term or even result in a marriage.

The issue of a woman's self-esteem is extremely important. If you are looking for a healthy, long-term relationship, failing to recognize a woman's level of self-esteem may mean years of problems for you, severe emotional pain, and even economic losses. The chances that a woman with LSE can change into an HSE woman, without years of therapy and a strong motivation on her part for change, are extremely, extremely low. Furthermore, the journey would be full of dangers for your own well being as a man. It is extremely important for you to learn to screen LSE women out of your life, and by doing so, make room in your life for HSE women.

10 Screening: HSE vs. LSE Women

What I need
Is a pretty woman next to me
To share the dreams that I believe
Maybe we could start a family
Someone who truly understands, how to treat a man
This is what I need — I Need A Girl (Part II), by P. Diddy & Ginuwine

EVERYONE screens. Men and women always screen for a potential partner and for a relationship, and they do so consciously and unconsciously. On the *conscious* level, we seek to find the features in our potential partners that we rationally believe will suit us the best. On the *unconscious* level, we are motivated by the magnificent strength of our biological and evolutionary drives.

Gender Differences with Screening

With regards to unconscious screening, nature has created an interesting mismatch between men and women. Men are especially driven by *visual* features when screening. It's important that you become fully conscious of that fact in order to be able to screen well.

Women, on the other hand, are particularly motivated by things such as a man's masculine dominance, social status and personality.

It's easy to observe the manner in which women screen, Just look at any internet dating site. Women typically present a long shopping list of the qualities they think they want in a man. Men do this too, but most men will admit — if asked privately — that what they are really hoping for is a woman that they find physically attractive.

Because of these differences in the screening process, men are usually completely unaware of how they present themselves to women.

As a man, the two most important things that you should understand about screening are that

1. Women are *always* screening you.

2. The way you present yourself will be the determining factor with regards to the women available to you for sexual relationships.

Tied in with your more visual nature as a man, you'll notice that when it comes to sexual partners, you appreciate *quantity*. In reality, there are probably hundreds of women within walking distance of you right now who you would find sufficiently attractive. If you're like most men, if the woman is physically attractive, available and not completely crazy, then you would be inclined to start some sort of a relationship with her.

Women, on the other hand, tend to be more concerned with the *quality* of mates they choose. This is not to say that women are on average any less promiscuous than men are; it is just that the criteria we naturally use when selecting a mate is fundamentally different from our female counterparts.

The problem that many men face is that they will often fail to screen for the personality of their potential partners. This is what women mean when they say "men think with their dicks." Women are very well aware of how primitive or instinctual men can be when they screen for women.

If the quality of your relationship is important to you, then you will want to avoid most situations with women who display too low self esteem (LSE). As we described in detail in the last chapter, only women with healthy self-esteem (HSE) are truly able to enjoy healthy relationships with other people.

It is important to discuss some of the pitfalls you will encounter with the screening, and how to recognize women with LSE. After you've mastered this skill, you'll be free to spend your time and energy on the multitude of HSE women that surround you. For motivation, let's examine some examples of poor screening.

Poor Screening: Two Classic Examples

One classic situation we see over and over again is the successful nice guy with a high sex drive who is only able to attract Materialistas by virtue of his material wealth, or Good Girls who view him as a potential provider and a fixer-upper "project." You can often spot such a man by his preposterous lack of fashion sense (as if his mother still dressed him), poor posture, passive-aggressive attitude with respect to women and relationships and generally deferential attitude towards the woman. His relationship with both the Good Girl and the Materialista is likely to be notable for its lack of hot sex, and by a substantial amount of drama. This situation occurs because he has been screening for women only based on his sexual drive with the Madonna stereotype present in his mind. (See Chapters 16 and 17 on the Madonna/whore Complex for more information on this point).

Another classic situation is the reformed player who would like to settle down but can't seem to find any Good Girls. Even the way he walks attracts Adventuress-type chicks and screens out the Good Girls, without him even being aware that it is happening. The reason for this is because the man lacks the skills necessary to detect aspects of a woman's personality which might actually qualify her as a good prospect for a more committed relationship.

In both these cases, these men are simply *not* screening women appropriately for what they really want, and they are suffering because of it. As are the women with whom they become involved.

More Examples of Poor Screening

All of these examples are based wholly on real situations.

Mom leaves Dad and the kids and runs off with the East Bay Rats motorcycle gang. Dad obviously didn't screen very well.

He was far too attracted to the good sex she was giving to him and forgot to consider her personality as a factor. And given that he had in fact scored an Adventuress, he didn't take advantage of this fact (wild sex, threesomes, etc.) while the taking was good.

Wife leaves husband, takes the kids, the house, the car, *everything*. This wife either has some Materialista in her, or she is seriously LSE, or perhaps both. Either way, husband didn't screen well enough. He was letting his Madonna/whore Complex and his visual sexuality affect his judgement and he did not see the *important* factors in her personality. Sir Paul McCartney is a recent example of this. No matter what kind of woman Heather Mills really is, McCartney certainly didn't screen for the type of woman he wanted.

Dad works hard to provide for his family, and when he comes home he wants some peace and quiet and happy, smiling faces surrounding him. Instead, his wife is constantly complaining about how awful things supposedly are. The man is baffled; as far as he can tell, they have a decent life and a healthy family. They should be reasonably happy, but instead, the wife is only able to focus on and magnify every little negative detail. While his wife may well be a Good Girl, she may also have low self-esteem and a relatively high, unfulfilled sex drive. This man did not screen for a calm, peaceful woman.

What should I Screen for?

Many men wonder about the type of woman they should screen for. This is the most important question, which most men will NOT answer truthfully. The most truthful answer is "What kind of woman am I capable of finding?" followed closely "What's available?" Most men don't have enough experience to even realize that asking such questions is critical, or feel guilt and shame for wanting to have the best relationships possible.

The reason that so many men do not ask "What am I capable of?" or "What is available?" is because most men do not have enough skills to meet a lot of women and seduce them. Instead of developing the skills, they settle for whatever they can get with their current skill set, or for what society and their peers deem acceptable. They reside in a world of *sexual scarcity*, making themselves much too easily available to women, whereas women operate from a position of *sexual abundance*. In other words, women tend to make themselves scarce so that men feel that they have to supplicate in order to get something from a woman.

The most important quality in a woman is how she treats you. If you cannot handle contentious, contrary women with a high sex drive, you had best screen them out. Women who have a high sex drive and have high self esteem will still give you lots of drama, to be sure, but it will be of a different nature. The HSE woman is giving you drama primarily as a means of continuously testing your strength as a man. The LSE woman, on the other hand, gives drama in a self-destructive and even vindictive and malicious fashion.

Most men, especially when younger, screen on looks alone. This is nearly always a mistake. As the old saw goes, "kissin' don't last like cookin'."

How she treats you

HSE women are able to love themselves and they do not engage in self-destructive behavior. She also demonstrates that she is capable of treating you and the other people in her life as well as she treats herself.

All women — both HSE and LSE — have a natural tendency to seek power over their men. However, an HSE woman will target your heart. This means that after having tested you for Alpha qualities, the HSE woman will try to gain rapport with you and achieve some kind of ownership over your mind and your feelings. On the other hand, the LSE woman will mainly use self-destructive drama in her quest to achieve power over you.

An HSE woman will demonstrate the skill to respect the borders of your ego. When an HSE woman tries to change you

— as all women will do to one degree or another — she will do so in a respectful way, from a frame of love and a sense of connection with you. She will often say things like, "I feel that we mean a lot to each other. I would love you to open up to me more". With an HSE woman, you will get the feeling that she wants to own your heart and mind, but in a non-violent way.

Conversely, an LSE woman will often invade the borders of your ego with severe drama or violence. In some cases, she will even be unaware that you have such borders.

An HSE woman's primary concern will be to gain rapport with you, while her own feelings will be of secondary concern. An LSE woman, on the other hand, will be continuously talking or complaining about how you make her feel, with little or no concern about gaining rapport with you.

We are aware that with this criteria we are screening out a lot of women in the western world today, but we do not care; we are more concerned with the safety and well-being of ourselves and you, the reader.

Now that you are clearly able to recognize women for their primary attributes, you are in a position to look beyond physical beauty and focus on true compatibility with your goals and desires. The great news is that once you develop these skills you will automatically become more attractive to women in general. Women find men who know what they want in life to be highly attractive. However, LSE women will now typically disqualify themselves from a relationship with you, because they start to recognize that they do not deserve a relationship with a man of your calibre.

How to Screen Effectively

The most important weapon in a man's arsenal of screening techniques is being able to control the frame of interaction, right from the beginning of the relationship. This is done most easily by "sweeping a woman off of her feet". A man that has the skills to meet, attract and lay a woman within a few hours smashes her Magic Pussy Syndrome and will have a window within which the choice of pursuing a relationship with the woman is at his convenience and on his terms, not hers.

This is 180 degrees opposite the cultural norm, where women choose not only for sex, but also for the relationship. We believe that in modern, western culture, this unilateral female power is deadly to successful, long-term relationships.

When we say that you should control the frame, that doesn't mean we want you to be a controlling, domineering jerk. It means we want you to know what you want and to be determined to not accept anything less than that.

In the long run, when a man does not know what he wants in a relationship, the woman will feel compelled to fill the leadership vacuum. If a feminine woman is forced to take on the role of leader within a relationship, she will inevitably lose attraction and respect for the man, sooner or later.

Eliciting Values

Understanding a woman's value structure is critical for evaluating the potential for a successful relationship. *Eliciting values* (EV) is a very useful tool that we can borrow from the field of neurolinguistic programming (NLP). The idea behind EV is to find out what is important to a woman, and what she desires in life and in her relationships.

The correct way to elicit a woman's values is to get her to talk about herself and her past relationships freely. This cannot be done if you are interrogating her in an interview style; rather it should flow through normal conversation. It will be helpful to put a woman at ease by revealing little tidbits about yourself at the same time, or at a minimum, displaying empathy and understanding for the things she is telling you.

It is also important to be completely non-judgmental when a woman is revealing details about her personality. If you reveal your standards and moral principles too quickly, it is a surefire way to have the woman either clam up completely, or to try to start painting an inaccurate picture of herself based on what she thinks you want to hear.

With experience, you will be able to quickly determine the woman's level of self-esteem by what she reveals about her past and current relationships. You will want to ask yourself continuously, is this a woman who sees the good in people under most circumstances (HSE)? Or is she someone who is constantly seeking to criticize and tear others down(LSE)? Is this a woman who tolerates and perpetuates physical, emotional, or verbal abuse (LSE)? Or is she someone who avoids abusive people and situations (HSE)?

Compliance

Once you are able to control the frame, you will quickly discover that LSE women are incapable of following you as the leader of the relationship, no matter how self-assured and in control of yourself you are. On the other hand, HSE women will find it much easier to admire and respect a man who displays such leadership qualities.

The way to distinguish between LSE and HSE women on this point is by mastering a technique called *compliance*. If you ask an HSE woman to do something for you, she may test you to see if you are confident enough to really be asking for the thing that you are asking from her. And an HSE woman will likely reject any request to do something that she considers demeaning or degrading to herself.

An LSE woman, on the other hand, will sometimes get angry and hostile towards normal, reasonable requests and she will often comply with degrading or abusive demands. If you do not wish to abuse a woman, you can simply ask about her past relationships, or put hypothetical propositions to her, and watch carefully how she responds.

The LSE Threshold Test

We spoke about the LSE Threshold Test in the last chapter but it bears revisiting. Why? Because screening women on their self-esteem is so important!

Start off by playfully joking with a woman, then move towards making mildly insulting comments, and go as far as you reasonably can. The point at which she objects to what you are saying indicates her threshold.

If you find that you are able to say things to a woman that make *you* uncomfortable by saying them, and the woman is responding either neutrally or by becoming sexually aroused, then you can be sure that the woman is more LSE than what your standards for a relationship will dictate.

Please note that under no circumstances do we advocate any kind of abuse in the context of a romantic relationship. The LSE Threshold Test is, however, an elegant mechanism for you to determine a woman's level of self-esteem when you first begin interacting with her. The test does not necessarily need to be run for very long or more than once. From there, you can decide whether you want to continue interacting in a normal way with the woman, or not. Furthermore, this test can be completely playful and non-judgemental, while at the same time subcommunicating your standards.

The Double Bind

One very effective means that you can employ to detect LSE women is observing the degree to which they demonstrate something called the *double bind*.

The essence of a double bind is the presentation of two conflicting demands, neither of which can be ignored, and which leave the victim torn between two options. The "options" are presented to the victim in such a way that whichever demand they try to meet, they find that the other demand *cannot* be met.

"I *must* do it (or say it) but I *can't* do it (or say it)" is a typical victim's description of the double-bind experience. For example, imagine trying to respond to a hostile woman, who is shouting at you, "I *know* that you don't love me!"

Psychologists have described the double bind as a pathologi-cal phenomenon. However, within the context of romantic relationships, it can also occur in situations which could be de-scribed as normal and to be expected.

The positive purpose of the double bind in human sexuality is to act directly upon the limbic system of the brain, so as to create a situation of confusion, which is meant to lower a lover's defense mechanisms, with the purpose of increasing the chances of sexual intercourse. Therefore, in spite of the painful nature of double binds, they can actually be a sign that your woman is becoming sexually aroused!

Well-adjusted people with healthy self-esteem will be able to get into situations involving the double bind, and back out again by employing normal, psychologically-healthy defense mechanisms. If a woman's use of double binds are rare and short-lived, then this is a good indication that she has high self-esteem.

On the other hand, if a woman is persistently and massively using double binds against you, and this is not connected with her becoming sexually aroused, then this is a clear-cut indication that the woman is LSE. This is because the behavior indicates that she is unable to verbalize the emotions connected with her sexuality in a mature, adult way.

Practical Advice

Much of proper screening results from having an appropriate self-image, and demonstrating your self-image in a way that effectively communicates to women what your standards are. The following advice will help you to naturally screen desirable women into your life, reducing the amount of effort to screen undesirable women out.

Being congruent, also known as "acting normal", is very attractive to women. When your internal self-image matches how women perceive you, that is called being congruent, and as a result, your attractiveness to the opposite sex increases. Sexual selection can then proceed. Women that aren't attracted to you will simply not appear in your life. Contrast this with the problem of breaking up with women you became involved with attempting to be someone you weren't.

Owning your own frame with sincerity is also crucial. If you really know and understand what it is that you want, you will find a large selection of women with the desire to bond with you, *on your terms*. Women in general just want to know what your terms are, whether you accept them as they are, and how likely you are to change your mind.

Having a man who knows what he wants is very comforting to women, while a man who doesn't know what he wants is a sexual turnoff and can even be frightening, especially to HSE women. Again, women without an appreciation for what you stand for simply won't be around.

The man who doesn't know what he wants, who cannot express his desire to women, puts women in a position of being responsible for the emotional content of the relationship. This will only be attractive to LSE women. And not only will unnecessary drama ensue, but a woman cannot feel at ease with a man who is so unsure of himself.

Having very high social value such that women clamor to be in your presence, is also something you want to cultivate carefully. A-List actors fall into this category. Freaky chicks (Adventuresses), who are primarily driven by external validation will certainly be attracted here. But HSE women across the spectrum of the archetypes are certainly attracted to men who have high social value. In this case, you must manage *all* of your relationships very carefully. What we do is manage our time, and don't allow women with romantic intentions, or anyone else, to waste our time.

Having a lot of money allows a man to select among a wide range of women with Materialista characteristics. The more the money, the higher quality the Materialista. Having a lot of money is also attractive to Adventuresses and Good Girls, but for different reasons. Any woman will be attracted to a man who displays the qualities of leadership, ambition, and self-reliance. HSE women will want to share the good life with you, whereas LSE women, with their tendency towards self-destructiveness, will sooner or later start to exhibit signs that they are poised to damage your material interests.

11 Stages of Manipulation

When it comes to marriage, one man is as good as the next. And even the least accomodating is less trouble than a mother. — Marquise de Merteuil in "Les Liaisons Dangereuses," by Choderlos De Laclos.

WE believe that manipulation is an instinctual behavior deeply rooted within female biology. Manipulation is also a *learned* behavior, due to one's need for survival. From a biological point of view there is not too much of a difference between biologically-rooted and learned behavior. In fact, from the point of view of both modern neurobiology and evolutionary psychology, behaviors repeated and learned over time become deeply rooted in the neurological patterns within the brain, to the point where the behavior becomes largely unconscious. As individuals are prone to choose behaviors which support survival, manipulation has certainly been selected as a desirable survival skill.

Manipulation can be defined as the attempt to influence another person's mind to achieve a certain outcome. Manipulation is very often seen as a negative thing. We, however, are not judgmental about manipulation, and actually consider it a positive feature, which has been designed to keep life continuing on this planet.

In order to best manage relationships with women, the Modern Man should understand that there are various *stages* of manipulation that a woman will go through during the course of a relationship with a man.

On the biological level, the female of our species is programmed to:

1. Elicit a strong sexual attraction in one or more strong males.

2. Feel a strong sexual attraction for such males.

3. Become impregnated by her choice of male.

4. Have a male to provide materially for both her and her infant child.

5. Afterwards, she will subconsciously tend to operate in such a way so as to have her sexual attraction for that male decrease.

6. Wash, rinse, repeat: she will tend to have more sexual intercourse and more children with other strong males.

We call this process *betaization*, where the strong, alpha male is rendered beta — which means "secondary" or "subservient" — within the relationship, over a period of time. Quite often, this process occurs gradually and almost imperceptibly to both parties.

Manipulation is widely used by women to achieve:

- Safety and comfort for her and her children, with their survival being the primary purpose.

- To thereby influence the man's mind in such a way that he will feel compelled to protect her and her children, especially before pregnancy, during the pregnancy and throughout the children's early developmental years.

Female manipulation can be either *creative* or *destructive*, depending on the desired outcome. From the point of view of the man, female manipulation can be considered "good" when it supports life and the man's interests and "bad" when it destroys life and/or damages the man's interests.

Succinctly, the more manipulation is used by a woman, the more it becomes natural and unconscious to her. It is like learning to play a musical instrument: at first it is difficult and one needs to pay conscious attention to each note being played. Then, as mastery is gradually achieved, manipulation becomes more and more unconscious.

Behaviors are slow to develop and also slow to be unlearned. In the modern woman of the industrialized countries, the way instincts are expressed has changed slightly with time, due to less-demanding survival conditions. However, the influence of the female's primal instincts on her behavior remains evident.

It is important for you to learn to recognize manipulation. In fact — as we discussed in Chapter 4 "Female Basic Conflict" — for a woman's sexuality to be satisfied, it is important that her manipulation attempts against her man *not* be too effective. You must learn to observe female behavior and give the right responses, with the goal of making her happy on the *emotional* level, as opposed to responding to manipulation attempts on a *logical* level.

Learning to respond appropriately requires knowing the various stages of female manipulation.

Stages of Female Manipulation

A woman's attempt to own you mentally will follow certain incremental stages, which predictably occur with mathematical precision. We will now discuss each of the following stages in detail:

- Testing the Male
- Seeking Communication
- Putting him to Work
- Evolutionary Selfishness
- Self-Determination

Depending on the woman's self-esteem, there are big differences in the way these stages will play themselves out. If a woman has high self-esteem (HSE), she will test you and manipulate you in a totally different way than a woman who has low self-esteem (LSE).

Testing the Male

"Let me be a little bitch to him." A woman knows on the instinctual level — and also on the rational level — that a man can impregnate a large number of women without too many consequences. In our modern age of mandatory child support, this is not always true in practical terms, but biologically it remains the case that the female has a much higher risk and burden when it comes to pregnancy than the man does.

A woman also knows that a weak male will not be able to protect her or her children in any way. Imagine as a man how your thoughts about survival would be different if every time you made love to a woman you faced the possibility of carrying a baby in your belly for the next nine months, followed by the primary responsibility of taking care of the baby for many years to come. Imagine how you would feel if you knew that your partner could leave you at any time and impregnate other women and/or leave for war or for hunting. Get the picture? You would become much more selective in your choices of who to mate with.

From this biological reality stems the deep need that a woman has to test the male for his physical and leadership qualities. In our modern society, the need to test for *physical* qualities and financial stability has become less important than the need for qualities such as leadership, intellectual capacity, and strength of personality; but that would be quickly reversed in the case of war.

One thing is for sure: a woman in this stage *will* test the male for his skill of being a hunter. This will happen whether you are skilled in hunting animals in the grassy field or company shares in the business field; you can be sure that at the first stage of manipulation a woman will test you.

A woman will *always* test a male who she is sexually attracted to. For a psychologically healthy woman, survival and sexual desire must always harmonize with each other. A woman who tests men *only* for survival benefits — such as a man's ability to provide — is denying her sexuality. A woman who tests men *only* for their sexual appeal, is either planning to live her life without men, or is being self-destructive.

Seeking Communication

"Open up to me, please."

Once a woman has tested the male, and is relatively sure that he is strong enough to serve her purposes, her concern begins to revolve around making the man serve her *exclusively*. Many men who are relatively strong and pass the tests of the first stage, fail to understand the meaning of this second stage. This stage is extremely difficult for the average man to detect. It is instinctually and often unconsciously masked by the woman as a purely innocent attempt to "communicate" with the male.

It is a feature of the feminine psyche to appreciate communication above all else, but from an evolutionary point of view what the female of our species is really doing at this stage is using language to *befuddle* her partner, which will hopefully cause him to serve her and her purposes.

This stage is extremely important to the success or failure of couple relationships. Couple therapy fails so frequently because it tends to disregard the real, evolutionary meaning of this stage. A very common pitfall for couples is when the woman starts to *feel* that the man is displaying an inability or unwillingness to "communicate properly" with the woman. Modern couples therapy almost invariably places the blame for this supposed lack of communication squarely on the man's shoulders.

In the first stage, the woman has screened out the weaker males; the man was specifically chosen by the woman for a relationship. In this second stage, the woman acts as if she is seeking deeper communication with the man. A strong man will start to sense that an attempt is being made to weaken him, and he will then usually react with certain predictable behavior patterns. He may get angry or he may withdraw. Arguments that seem to the man to be based on nothing logical at all will often occur at this stage.

Putting Him to Work

"Honey, please take out the trash and wash the cat, and please hurry!" When and if a man opens himself emotionally up to a woman — in the sense of what we discussed in the preceding subsection — from that point onwards the woman effectively owns the frame of the relationship. Now, the active destruction of attraction can begin in earnest, as she starts her attempts to take over aspects of the man's life which directly affect his material interests. For example, purchase decisions can now be made "jointly" which, in the cool light of rational analysis, really are the result of the woman's manipulation attempts and the man's desire to maintain some semblance of peace in the household.

Female Evolutionary Selfishness

"I am never satisfied no matter what you do or how hard you try." This stage begins once the woman has succeeded in having her formerly-strong male open up to her emotionally. In this stage, any communication with her male partner is only for the purpose of deriving something useful for her and her children. At this stage she will exhibit a total disregard for the man's psychological and material interests. The man will be put under the power of a strong and constant psychological double bind, along the lines of:

"If you don't open up to me I am not satisfied. You don't communicate with me."

simultaneous with

"As soon as you open up to me I will use the information you provide in a totally selfish way for my own needs."

Either way, the end result for the male is usually guilt, shame, or confusion, finally giving way to resentment and anger. Assuming he takes her seriously — and most men do — he will get caught into an ongoing psychological mechanism, which will make him weaker and weaker, with terribly-negative results for her sexual attraction towards him. At this stage, he is no longer the strong male she admired at the beginning.

Female Self-Determination

"I am full grown, independent woman now." Of course, the female in the relationship never was a "little girl." In the self-determination stage, however, another double bind — even more powerful than the preceding — will be thrown at the male. Once he starts to seek out the emotional communication that *she* had been asking for all along, she will begin to express sentiments such as she is feeling oppressed, or that the man is boring, or that he is too nice, or that he doesn't understand her, and so on. Again, the usual effect of such feminine expressions on the man is bewilderment, shame and guilt.

If at this point the man decides that he does not care at all about what she says or does, she will assert that "he is not a loving husband/boyfriend" or "I cannot live with him because he does not understand me," or "I do not feel anything for him anymore," or "sex without communication is a turn off"; once again inducing some very negative feelings within the man.

In the Self-Determination Stage, the female expresses her resentment and dissatisfaction with the relationship. This happens virtually without exception in the case of male partners who have become progressively psychologically weaker with time.

Men who are able to pass through these stages without a corresponding decrease in their women's sexual attraction towards them are exceptionally-strong men. These men avoid becoming psychologically weaker through the process. We believe that such men are more the exception than the norm. It is much better for nature to first create attraction between a male and a female and soon after have it decrease. That helps to ensure both a safe upbringing of the offspring as well as more sexual interactions with other sexual partners, which in turn results in more offspring and a wider spreading of genetic materials.

This is not much different from what happens with many animal species, including species where the female kills the male after copulation. In the case of humans, this "killing" happens on the psychological level. The killing of human males by their female partners is largely symbolic, but we must also take into account those men who take this process so seriously that they start to destroy their health through the abuse of alcohol or drugs, or start to abuse their partners, or even murder their partners or commit suicide.

In other words, permanently-monogamous sexual relationships are not necessarily natural. They are partly a modern, social construct. Or, put another way, they are a social construct, the evolutionary purpose of which lasts for as long as Nature considers it useful.

Manipulation End-Game

In traditional, male-dominated societies, if the female cannot leave the relationship when her attraction evaporates through the process discussed above, the end result is often clinical depression and/or cheating. Clinical depression occurs when her sexual attraction for her mate decreases or dies out completely, and she is prevented from having sex with other males by social restraint. The woman in this case has to face a practically impossible conflict between her emotions, which demand sexual satisfaction, and her societally-restrained behavior, which prohibits sexual satisfaction.

In modern, politically-correct societies, a common end result of the manipulation process is the woman ending the relationship, or acting in such a way that the man has no other choice but to end the relationship. Infidelity is very likely to happen in either case.

Psychological counseling and family therapy usually fail to help couples in this situation because they start from the shaky assumption that exclusive committed relationships are always "healthy" and that having sex with different partners is "sick." They also fail miserably in detecting the slow and dangerous psychological process whereby the mind of the male is confronted with schizophrenic double messages from the female, which would be considered to fit the clinical definition of *Bor-*

derline Personality Disorder by most experienced clinicians on the planet.

Usually what happens in therapy and psychological counseling in the western world is that the male is made to be the scapegoat of a process which has been actively maintained by the female. There are *some* professionals who understand this process better than most, but they often do not have the courage to speak out about it. On a meta-level, what is happening with this social process is simply another evolutionary mechanism, one which allows for more pregnancies and for the upbringing of children in the most viable way possible.

There is certainly a strong cultural influence at work here and it behooves men to understand these forces and to work hard to make themselves strong men who do not succumb easily to female manipulation. Above all, a man with children should start from the premise that he is an equally important and vital link to a child's psychological well being. There are countless studies which show that statistically, children do better in every social and psychological respect when they enjoy the equal influences of a healthy male and a healthy female parent.

Practical Advice

Although the onset, intensity and order of occurrence of each of these stages in the betaization process may vary from woman to woman, in our experience this process has occurred in *every* long-term relationship we are familiar with: ours, our friends, and our families, and in countless case studies that we have researched. In fact, this process is exactly the means by which women turn short-term relationships into long-term relationships. However, female manipulation is not difficult to counter once a man understands the process. Let's revisit each stage in turn.

Testing never ends. Women test unconsciously. Testing is the woman's primary method for determining *congruency* and for discerning a man's authenticity; his ability to be genuine. Testing ceases to be an issue of any significant consequence when the man is fully congruent — both internally and externally. The woman will still always test, but once a man has it together, he will pass the woman's tests without much effort or even realizing he is being tested.

Since testing is so closely related to the mechanisms controlling sexual attraction, it is important to remember that *testing never ends*. Maintaining an appropriate level of attraction within any romantic relationship is very important. One way we, the authors, maintain attraction with our mates is through regular, social interaction with other attractive females. For more information on why maintaining friendships with the opposite sex is important to your relationship, please see Chapter 19, "Male Qualities Attractive to Women."

Seeking Communication is really her signal that she is suffering from emotional ambiguity. Most men view a woman's pronouncement of "I don't feel we are communicating" as a logical statement addressing the exchanging of facts — or a lack of such activity — between two people. It is not. It is an emotional statement involving her confusion and emotional disconnection from the relationship.

When the woman puts the blame on the man, this is normal, for two reasons. For one, women habitually blame their own emotional distress on external factors, thus absolving themselves from responsibility. When a man happens to be the most convenient "blame receptacle", then he gets the blame. The second reason she does this is that she is actually making a request for masculine leadership. She wants her man to step up and deal with her out-of-control emotional state with masculine strength, and without fear.

The only important word in any such statement coming from a woman is "feel." It's so important that in many cases it doesn't matter *what* she feels, as long as it's any emotion stronger than indifference. Anything with passion will do, as long as it's followed up, in all cases, with the appropriate level of physical commitment. And always make sure that intense displays of passion are followed by intense displays of affection. Let's be blunt: keep her well-sexed.

Being Put to Work can be stopped simply by saying "no." Do it sometimes. Just say no! If your woman has become habituated to your instant obedience, then refusing a request is going to stop her in her tracks. She will literally not know what to do. Lots of drama could ensue, so be prepared.

Another way to handle her constant requests is in a spirit of teasing and fun. You can gently make fun of her being "bossy," and so forth.

Yet another effective way to handle a woman's attempts to put you to work is to *negotiate* with her. For example, if she demands that you take the kids shopping for clothes, you can kindly request that she prepare a special meal while you are gone. While tit for tat may seem thoroughly unromantic, by the time a man is in this situation, we believe the romance is far gone anyway. There is nothing to lose, and your self-respect to regain.

Best yet, *be proactive* and act like a leader: *women want to feel useful and contribute to something meaningful.* Spend some time to give your female counterpart meaningful work, ensuring that *you* are the one who determines the direction of the family. You will find that agreeing on specific tasks becomes much easier. When you appreciate a good woman for her specific contribution, she will be delighted in her relationship, and feel she made an excellent selection in a man.

Evolutionary Selfishness is understandable when we consider that the female's primary concern is always for her own well-being and that of her children. It is difficult — if not impossible — for most women to feel altruistic or merciful towards a grown man. Your role as the man is to be her protector, or to get out of her way. However, as a strong protector you have great value in the eyes of a healthy woman. So the key here is to assert your value and put a price tag on your leadership of her and the family. This means simply that you *lead* the relationship and continually give her tasks within the context of the relationship.

Putting a price to your leadership also means having your own moral standards, whereby it's subcommunicated from the beginning and throughout the relationship that you, as a man, expect certain behaviors and certain types of treatment from the female, if she is to retain your interest in being her leader and protector. As we discussed in the chapters on Screening and Female Self-Esteem, certain women, obviously, will *never* be able to submit to male leadership, no matter how strong you are.

Self-Determination This stage is a very strong signal from the woman that — in her mind — the relationship has ended, or is about to end. She is effectively telling you that she no longer views the two of you as a unit. As difficult as it may seem, at this stage you may need to be prepared to let her go. Your best chance to salvage the relationship may be to start right back at the beginning; let her know that you are equally prepared to leave the relationship if you are not getting the respect and admiration that you want and deserve.

You *never* want to be in a position where you are chasing or begging a woman. Not only is that a pathetic position for a man to find himself in, but any shred of sexual attraction that had remained in the woman will be completely destroyed by such actions.

In reality, a man can survive just about *anything*, including the ending of a cherished relationship. Therefore, consider this stage as the ultimate test of how much of a man you really are. If you fail this test, the game is over with this particular woman.

12 Root Causes of Conflict

You are the lovers rock
The rock that I cling to
You're the one
The one I swim to in a storm.
Like a lover's rock. — Lover's Rock, by Sade

MOST of us have been in a relationship where, at one point or another, we felt like we were engaged in a battle for power with our female counterpart. Certainly, we've all heard about such scenarios. In some cases the conflict can spiral into something downright nasty, such as verbal or physical abuse, resentment, guilt and shame, and finally, breakup or divorce.

It is important to note that *some* friction within a relationship is natural and can create a lot of good sexual tension, but only if it is handled properly.

In this chapter we will explain some root causes of relationship power struggles. We'll also teach you some techniques for managing the relationship to your mutual benefit, while helping your partner to have a lot of fun and good feelings in the process. The authors love women very much, and this chapter is about creating a positive outcome for everyone.

Root Causes of Conflict

In our view, there are three root causes of conflict in a relationship:

1. Improper Screening
2. Mishandling of Early Frame Announcements
3. Failure to Establish Boundaries

Failure to properly handle the above-three items is a death sentence for long-term relationships. The first two items always need to be dealt with *before* a serious long-term relationship is undertaken. Setting proper boundaries is an ongoing process, and the man that doesn't learn to set and insist on appropriate boundaries is running a serious risk as well. Let's now examine each of these root causes of conflict in more detail.

Improper Screening

Millions and millions of people marry the wrong person. Without a strong social fabric that binds marriages together for the life of the partners, while also allowing the husband and wife some respite from each other, life-long marriage is quickly becoming a relic from an incomprehensible age. Lacking a culture that provides a rational mechanism for choosing a mate, how does a man choose a suitable wife for a prosperous and peaceful life? He does so by first learning to screen women for the traits he finds desirable. And, *just as importantly,* he must form an understanding of the price he will pay for getting involved with a woman with such traits.

For example, do you want a really hot woman? One who is hot now, and will be hot when she is 40? Well, do you have the libido to keep up with her? Or the emotional maturity to manage her libido for her? Can you mentally and emotionally handle the thought of her being constantly hit on by other men, every time she leaves the house? If not, then you may find yourself much happier with a woman a little less "hot."

Female Integrity

To many men, the very notion of female integrity is an oxymoron of the highest caliber. Right up there with "military intelligence." However, we believe it's unproductive to hold women to the same standard of integrity as men, especially in the modern world where women are not held accountable by society in the same way men are. A better way to come to grips with female integrity is to "trust the woman to act as a woman."

For example, consider the female view of honesty and promises. Have you ever heard the aphorism "A woman is only as good as her word?"

Didn't think so.

There is a double standard here. Do we need to mention that women will break promises with impunity, yet call a man out for doing the same? When a woman makes a promise, it's because something made her feel a certain way. The reason for the double-standard is that when a woman makes a promise, this is what she actually believes to be true at the moment, based on her emotions. Later, when she feels differently, the promise is no longer valid. A promise from a man has a different meaning. Rational, or masculine integrity, standing by one's word, is a predominantly-male concept. In addition, in the desire to right many oppressions against women, women generally have far lesser consequences to lying under the law; thus, lying becomes a habit.

Summarizing, we trust a woman to act with her integrity as a woman, not with our notions of integrity as men.

The Early Frame Announcement

The Early Frame Announcement (EFA) is a verbal or sometimes non-verbal frame that a woman establishes in her first interaction with a man she is attracted to. Using the EFA, the woman subcommunicates exactly how she will place certain needs of her own as absolute preconditions for the relationship itself to exist. Sometimes this is done consciously, sometimes unconsciously. You can consider a woman's EFA to be a fairly rigid and inflexible statement of what she demands from the relationship.

Failure to detect the EFA can cost a man a lot of energy and possibly a lot material possessions. Therefore, understanding the concept of the EFA and being able to act accordingly are important skills for you to have. It's crucial that you can determine quickly — right at the beginning of an interaction with a new woman — whether it is wise to invest yourself into a new romantic relationship, or not.

When properly applied, an understanding of the EFA can spare you from a lot of trouble and heartache. It's important to always remember that, as a rule, most women will be totally inflexible with regards to their EFA, no matter how long the relationship may last.

A mistake that men often make is that they fail to take the EFA seriously. *The most important quality in a woman is the way she treats you as a man.* The EFA is usually a clear and unambiguous signal from the woman about the way she will treat you and why. So pay attention to it carefully.

Subcommunicating the EFA

It is important to understand that relationships are very important to women and that women have a compelling need to frame their relationships according to their emotional needs, which they reveal to us during the EFA. The EFA can also help us to determine what type of girl we are dealing with, as in Good Girl, Materialista or Adventuress, whether she is HSE or LSE, and in some cases, whether she is LD or HD.

Women will establish these EFAs from the beginning in a very sweet and subcommunicative way. They may not be direct. Few women are willing to expose themselves as Materialistas by bluntly stating "diamonds = sex," or as Adventuresses by flatly saying something like, "I party with the fastest crowd I can find." Consider the EFA like a "my way or the highway" frame, delivered in a sweet-and-silent, feminine way.

Accepting an EFA from a woman is a tacit admission that she has chosen you for a relationship. In extreme cases, she may demand not only very specific terms and behaviors from you, but she will predicate sexual availability on her EFA. In our experience, this is unworkable in this age of no-fault divorce. Even if not married, this makes it easier for her to break up on a pretext once whatever attraction there was dissipates, rationalizing with "The marriage wouldn't have worked anyway."

It cannot be emphasized too much that the EFA is something that all men should learn to listen for very carefully. In expressing her EFA, the woman is giving to the man a clear but subcommunicated message of her most important needs within the context of a relationship. It is vital to note that a woman will always put the needs that she expresses with her EFA above the man's needs. These EFA-expressed needs of hers are even more important to her than the man himself!

Detecting a Woman's EFA

Have you ever been on a first date with a woman and she starts prattling on about apparently random aspects of her personality or lifestyle? For example, she may say something like: "I am generous to a fault", and yet expect you to pick up the tab. Such incongruity preys heavily on the mind of most men, who don't understand that the women has just started dictating the terms of power in any forthcoming relationship. she has made an Early Frame Announcement (EFA).

The man that allows a woman to establish the entire frame of the relationship in such a manner, will most likely find that his needs come far, far behind the "needs of the relationship," which means, *her needs*. Worse, he will wonder "What the hell is happening?" as he feels in his guts that his masculine power is evaporating. Ever notice how when a woman says "We", your testicles seem to shrink?

Think for a moment about her statement, "generous to a fault." To whom is her generosity extended and why? How could anyone's genuinely-offered generosity be faulted? In this particular case, what she is subcommunicating here is "I, the woman, am going to do nice things, like arranging flowers for you, the man." Notice what happens if the man remarks that flowers aren't really his cup of tea. Because the woman established this martyr-like frame early on, she now has a mechanism for displacing all the responsibility for her bad feelings onto the man: "He doesn't appreciate anything I do." And she will use this like a whip to subjugate the male. We call this behavior "betaization," a process we believe is evolutionarily driven, inexorable, and largely unconscious.

The ramifications of unconditionally accepting a woman's EFA are many and varied, but all lead to the same end: the subjugated male. This is ultimately an unhappy result for the vast majority of men *and* women in relationships. (We don't speak for — or judge — those happy couples in fully role-reversed relationship where the woman dominates a submissive man.) From the current example, a woman who is "generous to a fault" will shower her man with unwanted gifts and attention, while using guilt and shame to manipulate his behavior.

Some Examples of the EFA

"My former boyfriend was aggressive and he abused me."
Translation: "I will be horny for you and appreciate you only if you will abuse me in the relationship."

Now, many will object to the translation shown above and say that we are being misogynistic, or worse. Perhaps the woman is stating that she unwittingly became involved with an abusive man and no longer wishes to have relationships with such a man.

Consider, please, the well-known psychological tenet that indicates we are attracted to certain types of people for a *reason*. People tend to repeat the same types of relationships over and over again in their lives. A woman may consciously feel she needs to stay away from abusive men and she may even know that these types of relationships are not good for her. But the fact remains that she accepted — and on some level enjoyed — a sexual relationship with a man of this nature.

We suggest that there is no way a woman would enter and remain in a sexual relationship with a man whom she does not feel a strong sexual attraction for, *especially* when there are aspects of that relationship which are clearly unpleasant. Sexual attraction is the core of a sexual relationship, and with her EFA, the woman is clearly telling you what type of men she gets sexual with, or, what personality she will eventually subconsciously try to extract from the men she gets sexual with.

In the translation shown above, many men have reported that this is precisely what happens when they find themselves in a relationship with a woman who has previously been in several abusive relationships. There will come a time when she will seem to be trying very hard to provoke a violent reaction from him. She may not be doing this consciously, but now you understand why this happens. The important point is that it is far easier to know and deal with this at the outset of a relationship, once the EFA has been delivered, than it will be later once you have already enjoyed sexual relations with her for a time.

"I like men who know what they want and take charge."
Translation: "I will relax and put all the responsibility for my life upon you, as soon as we start our relationship."

This kind of woman can be delightful to be around. Just be aware that she may also be extremely passive-aggressive, and perhaps depressive as well.

"I love jewels... they make me so happy!"
Translation: "In our relationship, I will demand material possessions from you in exchange for love and sex."

The classic Materialista. You've been warned.

"I often like to go dancing late at night. I don't understand people who like to sit on the couch and watch television."
Translation: "I want to have fun in any relationship and be out late at night, either with you, or without you. You can expect that I will frequently come home drunk from the club."

Warning: if you don't know how to handle a woman like this, you're asking for trouble!

"I just love to spend my time with my girlfriends after work. It is so refreshing to chat with them."
Translation: "I only want to have fun while I am with you. Don't even think to stop me from doing that when we are in a relationship together."

"I need my space in a relationship."
Translation: "I am the most important person in this relationship and you will have to practically beg me to get any affection or sex."

Be wary of attempting any sort of long-term relationship with a woman stating this EFA. An acquaintance of David's has been trying to date one of these "socially responsible" women, someone who has volunteered for service in a primitive nation halfway a around the world. Of course, she needed her space. His acquaintance finally wised up after several months and went out and scored some one-night stands at a local hotspot. He rightly figured he was being used as her backup boyfriend, in case she wasn't able to find someone of a more socially-conscious stripe during her service. Her later response went something like: "Well, I didn't think you actually would date other women!" That was a *gross* insult to his masculinity, and clearly shows her actual opinion of him: lovable loser, boyfriend of last resort, etc.

On the other hand, women stating this frame can make excellent partners for *friends with benefits* (FB) relationships. Which, in fact may be what they are actually looking for in the first place. Such women may possibly be married, or have a "real" boyfriend elsewhere. Who knows? Who cares? Enjoy this kind of woman for who she is and do not trouble yourself with investing too much of your time and energy into her. When she wants more from the relationship, be assured, she will let you know.

Setting Proper Boundaries

It is vitally important that you know what you want out of your life and what you expect from your relationships with women. You should not allow any feeling of neediness or desperation for a relationship to interfere with recognizing a woman's EFA and making it clear — at least to yourself — that your boundaries will not be violated.

It's important to realize that every human being is unique, and what is perfectly acceptable female behavior to one man may be unacceptable to another man. The point of learning to recognize a woman's EFA is not to judge her or think badly of her, but to make good judgments for your own time and energy. Therefore, one of the keys to maintaining power in your relationships is knowing what you want from women.

Given that there are literally billions of women on our planet, and probably millions within driving distance of where you live, there is simply no reason to accept bad behavior from the women you choose to invest your time and energy — and perhaps money — into relationships with.

It's important that a woman understands from the outset that you are a man who knows what his core values are in life and cannot be swayed from them. We are not talking about being intransigent or having an inability to negotiate or compromise in general, however, there should be certain principles in your life that you rarely violate, if ever. Let's say, for example, that you've decided not to do drugs. It would be completely inappropriate for you to violate this principle in an effort to appease your wife or girlfriend, in the vain hope of placating her.

To some extent, if you've made certain hobbies or friendships to be important parts of your life, you should never start to retreat from these things if your woman starts to give you grief about them. You might *think* that — when your woman is complaining about your friend Bobby — that she really wants you to curtail or eliminate your friendship with him, but more than likely, *she is subconsciously testing your inner resolve*, to determine whether you are a man who can be swayed by a woman's emotional manipulation, or not. This is counterintuitive but crucial! Making the wrong choices when it comes to your boundaries and your woman's attempts to push back on them can result in a loss of sexual attraction and *increased* demands from her.

Practical Advice

The easiest way to preempt a women's EFA is by simply being her Prince right from the start. Sweep her right off her feet. If she has chosen you for sexual engagement — and choosing for sexual engagement *is* the woman's prerogative — then you should take her there so fast that she is powerless to resist. Make her weak in the knees. Let her feel herself toppling into you. Give her an out-of-body experience, a seduction she can brag about to her friends: "I had no choice, I couldn't help it." If you don't have such seduction skills, acquire them. It's much less expensive to spend a couple of years and few thousand dollars developing seduction skills than it is to be married for years in an unsatisfying marriage, especially if the marriage eventually fails.[1] If you plan on being married one day, or are already married, or still married, as the case may be, learning *real* seduction skills will pay off. Just because Dear Wife is married doesn't mean she doesn't want to be seduced. Think of it the other way around: just because you're married doesn't mean you don't want a blow job.

Lacking a memorable seduction to kick start a relationship, the most important thing for establishing harmonious relationships with women is to use the EFA proactively. Set boundaries for both her *and* the relationship directly, whenever appropriate. Screen her behavior for general compliance. Louis and Copeland [9] refer to the entire suite of these activities as "managing [her] relationship expectations." The more intimate the relationship, the more the woman needs to earn her role in that relationship in order to be happy. No one values anything they get for free. When you price-tag your time and energy in this way, you are actually giving the woman a gift that most men are incapable of giving.

[1]Franco seduces his wife on a regular basis. David Clare seduces his girlfriend at least several times a month. Mr. South, well, Mr. South is just one of those kinds of guys.

13 Female Manipulation

The man is the head of the household, and the woman is the neck — Rev. Jerry Falwell

WOMEN MANIPULATE. This is sure as the sun rising in the east. Manipulation occurs because of inferior physical strength and centuries of male domination; it's women's source of power and they are generally very good at it. It helps them to feel like they are on more of an equal footing with men. Manipulation is largely subconscious; women saw their mothers doing it, too.

As noted previously, we do not make a judgement call about the moral content of manipulation, other than to say that manipulation is good when it furthers a relationship in a positive way, and bad when it is destructive to either partner in the relationship, or to the children within the structure of a family.

In this chapter, we describe many forms of manipulation employed by females, including manipulation that we have not seen described elsewhere. Along with our descriptions, we provide examples and suggestions for countering manipulation as it occurs.

Double Bind

The emotional Double Bind is one of the primary means used by females to manipulate males. It's a powerful psychological mechanism by which the female of our species commonly *binds* the mind of the male so as to have him invest his energy into her, with the ultimate purpose of procreation and the safe upbringing of her children. The primary effect of the Double Bind on a man's mind is to have him *puzzled*. A man will naturally try to solve any puzzle that is presented to him, and particularly if it involves a female that he is sexually attracted to. By so doing, he invests more and more of his psychological energy into the particular female. Another way to describe the effect of the Double Bind on the male mind is to induce "paralysis of analysis". In cruder terms, you can also think of the colloquialism, "damned if you do, damned if you don't," when it comes to the Double Bind.

Think, for example, of the following words, dreaded by men everywhere: "Does this dress make me look fat?" The correct, logical answer is probably yes, it does make her look fat; otherwise, she wouldn't be asking. If it does make her look fat, stating the fact insults her, but declaring that it doesn't make her look fat exposes you as a liar. Now you're in trouble; you're damned either way. No worries, we'll revisit this situation later in the chapter.[1]

Description of the Double Bind

The Double Bind concept was first introduced to the scientific world by Gregory Bateson (9 May 1904 - 4 July 1980). Bateson was a British anthropologist, social scientist, linguist, and cyberneticist whose work intersected that of many other fields, including psychiatry. Bateson described the Double Bind as a communication paradox, first observed in families with a schizophrenic member. A true Double Bind requires several conditions to be met:

1. The victim of the Double Bind receives contradictory injunctions, or emotional messages on different levels of communication (for example, love is expressed by words, while hate or detachment is expressed by nonverbal behavior; or a child is encouraged to speak freely, but criticised or silenced whenever he or she actually does so).

2. No meta-communication is made possible; for example, it is not permissible to ask which of the two messages is valid or to describe the communication as making no sense.

3. The victim cannot leave the communication field.

[1]Joseph: A cocky thing that I sometimes like to say in this situation is, "no honey, the dress doesn't make you look fat, your *fat* makes you look fat!" All the while, I will escalate the physical component of the interaction. This is a high-risk, high-gain move.

4. Failing to fulfill the contradictory injunctions is punished, for example by the withdrawal of love.

An Example of a Double Bind in Action

A woman will often say — in a dramatic and emotional manner — something along the lines of, "you don't understand my feelings!"

If the male qualifies himself to her and tries to understand why she would say such a thing, then she will invariably keep on repeating the frame: "You don't understand my feelings". She will do so in many different ways, so that the man will feel compelled to put more and more of his mental energy into her.

On the other hand, if the male does *not* qualify himself to her, she may repeat, over and over, something like: "You see, I told you, you do not understand my feelings!"

As Bateson describes, what will happen in such a case will be as follows:

1. Contradictory injunctions. No matter what the man says within the woman's frame of "understanding emotions," he loses. In fact, his attempt to even engage her on the topic in a logical manner *demonstrates* to the her he lacks fundamental emotional skills.

2. No meta-communication possible. Meta-communication is the psychological skill of analyzing and discussing different models of communication used between individuals. This skill is usually taken for granted among psychologically healthy adults, but as the woman shuts this possibility off from the male, he will face her Double Bind without any chance of discussing its content with her.

3. The victim (feels he) cannot leave the communication field. This is because the Double Bind causes the victim to invest ever-increasing amounts of psychological energy into the person delivering the Double Bind.

   When the Double Bind is used within the context of a romantic relationship, it assumes important biological and physical aspects. Human males are strongly driven towards the female by both visual sexual attraction *and* the need for affection. Therefore, when a woman uses a Double Bind, the man is not usually motivated to withdraw; instead, he often becomes motivated to invest even more energy into the relationship.

4. Failing to fulfill the contradictory injunctions is punished, for example by the withdrawal of love. This is counter-intuitive.

   Once a woman has caused a man to invest his psychological energy into her by means of the Double Bind, he is now in a very vulnerable position. She can now easily make the man do whatever she wants, and she can punish non-compliance with the withdrawal of her affection and sex.

In the long run, allowing Double Binds to proliferate within a relationship is enormously destructive. Failure to understand and properly handle double bind manipulation can have an extremely-destructive effect on male self-esteem. Repeated use of the Double Bind by the female becomes a lose/lose situation for *both* parties: he loses his self-esteem, while she loses respect for him. Over time, a woman can become completely demotivated to be altruistic to the man in any way, because by dominating the man's mind, he progressively loses any evolutionary value he may have had in her eyes.

What follows are more examples of Double Binds:

"I need a man who is comfortable talking with me, who is able to express his feelings"

together with

"Men who talk too much are wussies."

"I don't like really muscular men, they are usually too egotistical"

together with

"A man without big muscles is surely a wussy."

"I want a man who knows how to lead me and make me feel secure"

together with

"I want a man who respects my freedom and does not try to boss me around."

"I go only go out with a certain type of man..."

together with

"unless I'm in love, then all bets are off."

By delivering such contradictory messages, a woman intends to have the man invest his energy into arguing with her about the content of what she said and then, following the pattern of the Double Bind, she will try to induce guilt and anxiety in the man. Note that each of the messages above simply reflect the woman's feelings at the particular time she was talking. Keeping that in mind goes a long way towards being able to handle the logical contradictions inherent in Double Binds.[2]

Practical Advice: Breaking the Double Bind

There is a very effective way to negate the effect of the Double Bind. It is not nice, fair or democratic, but it is the only method that works consistently.

The rule is that you must recognize that every Double Bind has some specific content. Then, you must refuse to buy into frame set by the content. For example, as in the examples listed above, the content could "listening/not listening to the woman" or "having/not having muscles". *You must, therefore, reject the content itself.* For example:

Woman: "You never share your emotions with me!"
Franco: "Yeah. So scratch my back please!"

Notice that the above conversation sounds exactly like an interaction which might occur between two schizophrenics. Here,

[2] Remember: the vast majority of women manipulate unconsciously, and without malice. Be the man that can look past the double bind, seeing it as an expression of some underlying emotion the woman may not be comfortable discussing, or may not even be aware of.

Franco simply does not buy into the frame of the Double Bind. At this point, women will divide themselves into one of three groups:

1. Some women will react to the man's adept handling of the Double Bind with increased sexual desire.

2. Women who are for one reason or another *unconsciously* suppressing their sexual receptiveness, and especially if they are intensely seeking a Provider, will simply cut their interaction with the man at this point.

3. Women who are *consciously* trying to suppress their sexual attraction — perhaps because of political ideology or because they are seeking to extract money from the man — will either change their attitude and become friends with the man, or cut off their interaction with the man.

As a man, this is exactly what you want! You want sexually receptive females to stick around, and you want the sexually non-receptive females to either disappear or simply become your platonic friend.

Breaking a Double Bind requires taking the frame of interaction back from the woman, and then emotionally leading her away from the arena of conflict.

Another effective way to do this is to not get upset but to *accept* her emotionally-driven assertion, *then* use male logic in an impudent way. If this produces a sharp emotional reaction in the woman, *then* escalate sexually, if logistically possible and if you so desire. Actually, it is highly impudent to escalate sexually at a seemingly inappropriate time, and that can often work very well. Once the woman's mind turns to sex, the Double Bind becomes irrelevant. Continuing with our opening example:

Woman: Does this dress make me look fat?
David Clare: Yeah, a big fat butt, that's what I like, gonna get me some big fat butt (pets her butt). [3]

[3]Note well: this works for David Clare because he likes his woman's butt just the way it is, something she can feel in his words and touch.

AB Indecision

AB Indecision is one way a woman will test a man on his leadership skills. She can also use this as a signal to him that she is "officially" turning over control to him, provided he is man enough to take it. This situation comes up when a woman feels insecure about a man's ability to lead. Here is what it sounds like:

Wife: Let's go out to eat.
Man: Sure, where would you like to go?
Wife: Oh, I don't know.
Man: (A) How about seafood?
Wife: No... too many calories... (whine whine)
Man: (B) Ok, we'll go to a salad bar.
Wife: (Indecision) Ooohhh... I just went there a few days ago and some "thing" happened that made me feel bad (she blames the environment for her emotions).
Man: (Starting to lose patience... wife won't tell him what she wants.) Well just tell me what you want!
Wife: Well fine! If you're going to act like that, I don't want to go out anymore.

If you recognize yourself here, you know that drama will now ensue, for no discernible reason. Bad feelings will develop, old wounds will be reopened, and in the worst case, incidents like this can trigger the resumption of huge conflicts.

Let's try this again.

Wife: Let's go out to eat.
Man: Sure, where would you like to go?
Wife: Oh, I don't know.
Man: (A) How about seafood?
Wife: No too many calories.
Man: (B) Ok, we'll go to a salad bar.
Wife: (Indecision) Ooohhh... I just went there a few days ago and some thing happened that made me feel bad.
Man: Well, I'm hungry, and I'm going to get some pizza. You're welcome to join me, or not, but I am leaving now (grabs coat).

Now, it is absolutely critical for this man to go get some pizza. She will probably — at the last minute — grab her coat and go with you. If she doesn't, *do not bluff!* Leave her at home to sulk. Bring her back a piece of pizza. If she apologizes, you are on the right track. If she spurns it, simply throw it away and ignore her. She will probably ask later where it is; tell her you threw it in the garbage, and go to get it for her out of the garbage. It's absolutely critical to hold your frame completely. No matter what she says about the pizza (too fattening, too greasy, she ate it for lunch, whatever), just go. She can sit and watch you eat. If she suddenly gets hungry, make her get her own food, or make her work for a bite of yours. In other words, *price-tag it.* For example, if she does something nice, she gets a mushroom, or a pepperoni. At this point, you have the frame, and she is yours to do with what you will.

Does that still sound like too much work? Good, because it is. Let's try a third time:

Wife: Let's go out to eat.
Man: I like the way you think. Grab your coat and keys, you're driving.
Wife: Where are we going?
Man: (Spins her around) We'll know when we get there!

The man in example one failed miserably is because he made some critical mistakes. First of all, he expected the woman to take the lead in decision-making, something that most women are loathe to do. Secondly, he tried address her emotions with logic. The woman was trying to communicate "Let's have fun!" and/or "I'm hungry!," with the expectation that the man would provide her with this, while the man was busy arguing over her emotional state.

In the second example, the man still failed to provide her with the good emotions she was seeking, but at least he avoided arguing logically with her regarding her emotions.

As you can see, the basic structure of AB Indecision is when two or more "choices" — both equally agreeable to the man —

are disqualified by the woman on emotional rather than logical grounds. Once a man learns that statements such as "Let's go out to eat." really mean "I'm bored, entertain me!", then these kinds of situations can actually be quite *enjoyable*, because they provide opportunities to play. Once you have mastered this, when a woman says "Let's go out to eat!" you will hear "Let's play!"

Bait and Switch

The Bait and Switch probably costs more men more grief than any other technique in women's arsenals. Succinctly, the Bait and Switch is just what it sounds like: offer something of value, then switch the valuable thing to a worthless thing once the hook is set. Women are very cognizant about this tactic; it has even been written up in *Cosmopolitan* magazine as a sure-fire way to get a guy interested in a relationship. So how does it work?

It's pretty simple. Did you ever know a guy that stated mournfully "My wife used to be so into Trucks/Camping/Beer Bonging before we got married. Now, she gives me a huge ration of shit whenever I want to do it, and I don't care if she comes along anymore." Bait and Switch, gentlemen, Bait and Switch. Wifey baited with some fun activity, set the hook (pussy), then removed it once she got what she wanted (marriage, or a committed, long-term relationship).

This works so well because so many guys have this fantasy of women as "dudes with tits." That is, they want male-oriented companionship, but with a woman whom they can have sex with when they get horny, instead of jerking off. We suspect that this fantasy runs very strong in men lacking normal socialization, and possibly among many otherwise-normal men as well. Natural ladies men know better than this, understanding that women are best enjoyed for their unique, womanly charms, and not to provide emotional validation equivalent to male bonding.[4]

It is important to note that the Bait and Switch is also a female test to detect weaker males, or weaker-male behavior. We have observed an increase in sexual desire in many females when the male is not effected by the mental power of the Bait and Switch. Therefore it is very good business for a man to learn to deal properly with this female mechanism.

Detecting the Bait and Switch

How do you know when the Bait and Switch game is afoot? When a woman shows apparently-sincere interest in something you do for fun, something you do that occupies your time away from her. Are you a surfer and she has never surfed in her life, but now, she has a sudden, overwhelming passion to surf? Watch out, buddy, because this is *exactly* how a Bait and Switch is set up. If you must, take her out on a special trip once in a while, make sure to show her lots of affection, and bone her silly afterwards. But take her only once in a while. Interestingly, a recent issue of *Surfer Magazine* had an article on this very topic: How to take a surf trip with your girlfriend. Their advice: pretty much same as ours.[5]

Breaking the game is easy once you can recognize it: simply treat any excursion as a normal date and plan accordingly. Make sure that is just uncomfortable enough for her that she won't want to do it again, but that the discomfort is from her lack of experience, from being out of shape, or from anything at all other than some way to blame you. And no matter how shitty

[4]Joseph: In industrial Canada, female competition for good Providers is fierce. The men do a lot of physical labor but make very good money doing it. It is not a coincidence that a majority of young women here are extremely-avid hockey fans.

[5]David Clare once dated a woman who had a wild, kinky side to her. He fell in love with her! Well, it turns out that part of her kink was *the chase itself.* Once she "caught him," the sex dried up, literally, and she started pressuring him about "the relationship." He figured out that, since the great sex was steadily diminishing as the level of commitment increased, he would promptly break up with her. He explained that he had already been through the Bait and Switch with his ex-wife. Her response: "That bitch! Your bitch ex-wife ruined you!"

it is, with crappy weather, filthy conditions, or whatever it is that bothers her, make sure that you absolutely revel in those conditions! You love being hot, cold, dirty, tired, thirsty, hungry or whatever, right? Have a great time! This will allow her to respect you, and to politely limit her future involvement. You can reinforce this by making sure to invite her out again once in a while, when the conditions are equally shitty.

An even better way to break the game is simply smile and nod: "Sure baby, I would love to take you climbing," but never actually do it. Or, drag it out and make her really, really work for the privilege. Once your inner game is locked on, you won't want the woman around for these activities anyway. It won't be validating to have her there; it will simply be a pain in the ass.

Ambush

A man works hard to provide for his family, maybe in a job he dislikes. The hardworking man then commutes home. Maybe the train is packed full of people, or the traffic is snarled. The hardworking man opens his door wanting nothing more than a few moments of peace and quiet. But he knows there is a top-level predator in his home — a female of the species *homo sapiens* — lurking in ambush, near the door. She has been "waiting all day" for the hardworking man's return. She is full of unspent emotion and lists of things for him to do. Her emotion must be dissipated immediately. The man must be put to work immediately. The hard working man's stress level rises another notch. He knows what is to transpire: As soon as his shoe crosses the threshold, she will launch herself at him with a litany of complaints and incessant chatter about meaningless aspects of her uneventful day.

It happens every day. He feels powerless.

This is unacceptable. A man's home should be his castle. A place of peace and refuge. But, what to do?

A woman's emotionality is compelling. A woman — and especially a modern woman — often feels that she has the absolute right to express her emotions freely, regardless of the opinions or reactions of those around her. This is especially true with regards to her romantic partner.

Especially with women with a high sex drive (HD), the approach of "Please let me rest when I come home from work" is not likely to be too effective by itself. This very-understandable male demand will usually face resistance from the woman. A woman understands — subconsciously, in her deeper, biological level of instinct — that if she does not comply with his demand, he will be forced to either:

1. Get angry with her. This will betaize him, though not as badly as can be expected under some alternatives. She will use his anger to to try to make him feel guilty about "treating her badly". In worst-case scenarios, she may use his reactions to try to demonstrate that he is mentally abusive or that he cannot control himself.

2. Start to qualify to her about her demands. This move is *totally* betaizing. In this case, in order to achieve peace at home, he will have to pay a heavy price to her, such as do favours for her, and comply with her demands for attention. In this scenario, men who are often completely Alpha at work end up in a completely Beta position at home.
3. Abandon his territory to go "hunting". This man will usually end up doing business all the time, or will spend a lot of time in the apartments of the other women he has hunted.[6]

4. Become a tyrant. As a man, you may very well feel that it is not fair or right for a man to not be able to relax in your own territory — your home — after you've done all you can for your family and your woman. Many men go

[6]Franco: I remember a man whom I coached who had slept at his place of business for ten years! His wife had the habit of giving him constant emotional outbursts while he was driving his car, with every single change in direction. At home, this man could not move a thing without having to face drama.

through a difficult moral struggle on this point once they realize that being polite and considerate is not having any effect against the Ambush.

It is important to understand that this female behavior seems to have deep biological roots based on primary survival instincts. For many years now, the dynamics of family therapy and counseling has made men feel guilty for supposedly not grasping the female need for communication. In fact it is true that a man should understand a female's need for communication, but that does not mean he should comply with manipulation or forfeit peace and quiet on his territory. Our policy has been to show understanding of the female need for communication, but *only* when the process of the communication does not indicate an attempt at manipulation or an ambush against our peace in the home.

The male biological brain structure is such that relaxation and silence during the times between battles and hunting are vital needs. When a woman tries to keep a man from doing that, she is in effect manipulating him when he is at his weakest point.

Some Practical Help: Focus on the Process

Men suffering from the Ambush are in a difficult position. Any attempts to negotiate the issue of your need for tranquility in the home may encounter resistance from her. Democratic-style discussion usually does not work. Instead, tell her your need for silence and relaxation on your territory and establish simple guidelines and rules within your household with regards to that. Verbal appreciation and physical escalation (if you have energy for that) may help reduce the drama, especially if you as a man are able to very rapidly dissipate her emotional tension.

If such efforts prove fruitless, find for yourself a couple of hours of relaxation with your friends in bars or restaurants before you finally go home. Franco does this with good success, finding that once he has relaxed from the work day it is much easier to emotionally engage at home. Another great method for minimizing the impact of the Ambush — if you can afford it — is to have more than one apartment or at least a private room that is totally separate from the rest of the home. Your studio or library should become a place dedicated to relaxation and peace of mind.

It is vitally important that you focus on the *process* of your verbal interactions with women, much more so than the *content*. If you are unaware of the process — which can happen when you get caught up in the specific words that a woman is saying — you can quickly become betaized.

Jealousy

New studies about jealousy seem to indicate that it is a strong, primitive instinct, which is meant to increase competition for sex between individuals. In other words, it is preserved in evolution because it has the positive purpose of increasing pregnancies. It is similar to what is achieved by the sensations of thirst or hunger in that it is designed to preserve human life.

The emotion of jealousy can therefore be viewed in a positive light, since it is meant to motivate people towards procreation. It is, in fact, crucial that you frame the emotion of jealousy as something natural and even positive. A man who is unable to put jealousy in proper context puts his emotional safety, his mental health and possibly even his assets at great risk.

Jealousy is widely used by females — whether consciously or not — as a means to control her male love interest. This is connected with her drive to maximize the profit she can gain by having a man fall into the role of Provider with her.

One especially common case you'll notice is that women will tend to create for you mental images of competition with other men. For example, a woman will often describe interactions with other men in vague ways, such that you start to really wonder whether she has any sexual involvement with these men, but you are unable to logically conclude it either way. She will usually do this in a subtle, even unconscious manner.

In this way, she is acting upon your strong instinctual drive to procreate. Women will tend to do this at all stages of a relationship.

It should therefore obvious why — if you are not able to properly handle your jealousy instinct — a woman you find attractive will easily be able to manipulate you into doing what she wants, such as marry her or support her financially, whether or not doing so coincides with your own best interests.

An important point to note here is that we are talking about *mental images*. These images do not necessarily mean that women will cheat on you. They simply indicate that you have been actually hypnotized by the woman's use of language, such that you find yourself in an altered mental state. You may very well start to feel that in order to be able to procreate with the particular woman you will have to please her, so as to avoid her being impregnated by other men.

Realize that it is the instinct of preserving life in you which can put you at the mercy of the woman! The positive drive towards the preservation of life is acting upon you. Allow yourself to feel the emotion of jealousy, but do not let the hypnotic effect of the woman's words affect your better judgement!

Rich Descriptions

Words can have a hypnotic effect on the brain. This has been demonstrated by science by measuring the effects of auditory stimulation on brain activity, magnetic resonance and positron emission tomography.

Our experience in dealing with women matches that of many professional hypnotists: the richer you describe an experience to another person, the more you will have that person actually *live* and *feel* that experience for themselves.

A Rich Description is a distinctive trait of femininity. Men, — especially very masculine men — communicate primarily by exchanging data. They tend not to use redundant, Rich

Descriptions. Men can enjoy spending hours exchanging facts but they will not usually enjoy richly describing them.

For example, a man who wants to talk about his experience at the gym with another male friend will typically express it like this:

"I was at the gym. I had a hell of a workout tonight!"

On the other hand, a woman talking about her experience at the gym might describe it more like this:

"Yesterday I was feeling so tired and depressed. Then I noticed my gym bag, the red one my aunt Mary gave me as a gift, and I started to remember how good I used to feel when I was exercising regularly. I started to feel like I wanted to get moving again! I used to be so much happier before when I was in shape! It was such a miserable, cold winter day yesterday, so I felt like I had better go to the gym."

The purpose of the female's use of Rich Descriptions in nature is linked to her need to manipulate her environment for the purpose of survival. By using Rich Descriptions in her conversations with the members of her social circle — and especially the males — she achieves the hypnotic effect of having those close to her desire to support her in her aims.

It is very important for you to recognize the hypnotic effect that female Rich Descriptions can have on the brain and to be ready to manage these effects within yourself. Again, your mental health and your assets can be put at risk if you do not!

Pouting and Whining

Pouting and whining are somewhat softer forms of manipulation seen in mammals. For example, dogs and cats clearly whine, and a pretty good case could be made that they engage in pouting as well. Both pouting and whining indicate a fundamental secession of authority, but they also represent of test of resolve. Whining comes from a place of weakness. Capitulating to whining comes from a weaker place yet. So don't do it.

Both pouting and whining are easily dealt with by teasing, as well as appreciation. It is important that you do both at the same time. On the one hand, the woman has turned over her personal authority to you, which should be appreciated. On the other hand, the point under consideration is probably in nobody's best interest, no matter how good it might feel to her to express her point in this way.

If the rest of the relationship is in order, then handling pouting can be as easy as this:

Her: "Whine whine pout pout" (The actual words are irrelevant, because her lower lip is stuck out)
You: "You are sooo cute when you pout!" (pinch her lower lip)

Practical Advice: Taking Action

One of the best ways a man can take action when being manipulated is using his birthright, which is his natural male logic. Women aren't stupid; they can use logic as well as men. David Clare knows many female engineers and scientists, most of whom are quite good at logic. However, they usually don't choose to use logic in *relationships*, because emotions work so much better for getting them what they want. When they use logic, they run a risk of losing the battle with their male counterpart.

In any case, if the man's logic is good, and doesn't hurt the woman's material interest (it may confound her desire, greed, or whatever), then a normal, healthy woman will recognize it for what it is and, we believe, respect the man for using it. This will be the case even if she gets upset in the process, so long as the man retains his composure.

So many times we have heard women say, "I want a man who is smarter than I am." We believe this — in part — means his ability to use logic in the sense we describe.

The key to using male logic requires two preconditions, both equally important:

1. Only apply logic to situations with a clear train of casuality, such as physical situations where B is clearly the result of A. For example, not paying bills results in calls from the collection agency, no matter what her "feelings" might be about bills, collection agencies, or whatever.

2. You as a man must be completely unengaged in the outcome. You must not care at all what she thinks or says about the situation. If she displays an emotional outburst to deflect her feelings or absolve herself from blame, you must absolutely retain your composure. In these situations, her opinion simply does not matter. Let her dissipate her emotion first, *then* you can engage her rationally.

This may sound unduly harsh. But there is big difference between really caring for a woman, and appeasing unacceptable behavior. The result is that you as a man will be able to provide necessary emotional strength to her, as she deals with emotions ranging from anger and embarrassment, to shame and disappointment.

14 Female Arousal and Sex Drive

Love to think that you couldn't love another
I can't help it... you're my kind of man
— *Bathwater*, by No Doubt

WE purposely put this chapter after the other chapters on screening, for several important reasons. First of all, sex is absolutely the core of any romantic relationship. In fact, we would go so far as to say that without a good sex life, you simply no longer have a romantic relationship, or at best, it is in a comatose state. Lack of sex that is satisfying to both partners in a relationship, however, is actually a symptom of deeper problems within a relationship. Later in the book, we will discuss important aspects of the male personality, which you can work on and improve, and in some cases even salvage a relationship that has gone sour. But it is certainly better to understand the type of woman you are dealing with *before* you become romantically involved.

Biological Differences in Sexual Drive

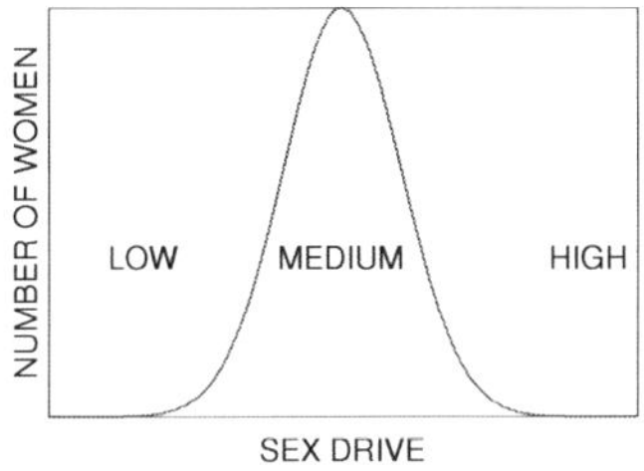

Before going any further, we emphasize that the material in this chapter generalizes and stereotypes women into what we consider extremely useful end-member categories on a spectrum of sexual drive ranging from Low-drive (LD) to High-drive (HD). In reality, very few women occupy the end member positions in this spectrum. We assume that sexual drive is normally distributed (as shown in the figure) and that most women have tendencies towards LD or HD. We have also observed that the same woman may be either LD or HD depending on circumstances such as environment, her age or time of life, potential partners, relationship status, and stage of relationship. Some women will always be well to one side or the other in this spectrum. Calibrate to the woman in front of you.

Just as the woman's sex drive is variable, so too the man's. The vast majority of men and women are more "medium sex drive," differing more in a relative sense than an absolute sense. In a relationship, more than likely the importance of HD/LD depends on where the man and woman are with respect to each other. For example, both the woman and the man may have lower than normal sex drives compared to the population at large. But one or the other will invariably have a sex drive higher than the other, and that's where the juice is. As you read through this chapter, keep this point in mind, understanding that most likely, whether the woman is HD or LD has as much to do with *your* sex drive as with hers. And as much to do with your ability to arouse her romantic urges.

When evaluating female sexuality, men often forget that the woman is the one to get pregnant and carry children. Men are prone to project their own sexuality on the woman, feeling that a woman would feel and behave like a man in that regard. In so doing, men tend to forget that the main biological purpose of human sexuality — unromantic as it may seem — is pregnancy.

Low Drive vs. High Drive Women

In this book, we divide women into two rough groups:

1. HD women. Women with a relatively stronger sexual drive.

2. LD women. Women with a relatively weaker sexual drive.

HD women are evolutionarily and biologically programmed to get pregnant more easily. They are programmed to make more children but at the same time to be inferior mothers. LD women are programmed to be better mothers and yet less prolific in the matter of pregnancy. Our theory has absolutely no moral implications; it is simply a strategy of Nature to spread its investments into different directions, as it usually does in the evolutionary area.

Women who are HD tend to get aroused sexually by verbal stimulation and male dominance very fast, and at a very high degree. On the other hand, women who are LD need a much longer time and greater verbal stimulation to achieve the same degree of horniness. This is purposeful from Nature. The faster way in which HD women get aroused by verbal stimulation — and their tendency towards dramatic emotions — means that those women are more prone to get pregnant. On the other hand, LD women may need a huge amount of verbal stimulation and a much longer time to achieve the same degree of horniness. This makes LD women less dramatic and more dedicated to childcare.

One could say that HD women are more *deliverers* and LD women are more *care givers.* This is one of the biological reasons that the M/w Complex (Chapter 16) was invented in the first place: a male projection of the fear of HD women, and of the illusory sense of safety given to them by LD women.

Low Drive Women

Many LD women are very much under the influence of what we like to call the frame of "the knight coming from afar." They are in a continuous state of preparing their hearts for their prince, whom they imagine as traveling great and difficult distances to come conquer the group and lead everyone within it. The worst mistake you can do with this kind of woman is to put yourself in the role a man who she has figured out completely. Instead, if you frame yourself as someone *rare, exclusive* and *difficult to reach,* and you maintain that frame at all times, then you can slowly influence a woman into more of an HD frame. How do you do that in practical terms?

Our method is simply that you reduce the time you are with her. Think: short, quality time. Give vague answers to her questions. Keep longer breaks between interactions with her. When she asks about what you do, you can use these James Bond-style cocky but funny frames. For example:

- "I was on a mission"

- "I had someone to take care of.."
- "I was flying to X"
- "I was flying from Y"

Note that this *James Bond frame* is not simply *saying* these words. The words themselves convey only 7% percent of the meaning. Your tonality and body language must convey those James Bond attributes: *Excitement! Adventure! Danger! Sex!*

In other words, you want to keep yourself in a frame where you are seen by the LD woman as:

- Mysterious.
- Always coming and going to and from places where she cannot reach you.
- Ambiguous and vague.
- Generally unavailable.

Unlike Franco and Joseph, David has a penchant for relatively LD women. David creates these kinds of interactions naturally by keeping a certain amount of his activity relatively close to the vest. Prematurely revealing intent before action may result in two situations conducive to reducing attraction. The first is that demonstration counts, talking doesn't. The second is that most men will collapse in the face of female disapproval of their behavior. Keep your failures to yourself until the pain has passed. Keeping the mystery alive allows you to surprise her with success, instead of disappointing her with big talk and subsequent failure.

Contrary to this frame would be deeply sharing all of your ongoing activity, allowing her to *feel* both success *and* failure. There is great power here, under the condition that you are not supplicating for her approval of your activities, and that failure results only a powerful, shared emotional experience, not a complete masculine frame collapse. In other words, feel free to share anger, disappointment and pain, but take full responsibility, without ever whining. Given most women's adroit capability for offloading responsibility, she will surely find a way to shift the blame from you to someone or something else. Let her.

Remember, once you are in a relationship with a woman, she *wants* to be attracted to you. Let these qualities emerge from within you; do not use them as manipulative techniques to compensate for emotional weakness, neediness or approval-seeking. If you do, your outward appearance will eventually collapse into your weak, hollow core, and your soon-to-be ex-girlfriend will complain that you weren't *genuine*.

High Drive Women

Two critical aspects of the HD woman must be understood. The first is that HD women crave being seduced and feeling masculine power just as much as LD women. The second is that drive and seducibility are not necessarily correlated. Some woman are easier to seduce than others, irrespective of their sex drive.

Due to the Madonna/whore complex, the The HD woman's strong sexual drive has long been a taboo in our culture. The figure of the HD woman has always been identified with the figure of *the whore*. This kind of woman has inspired fear in men; fear of them not being able to satisfy her sexually and emotionally, and fear of the extreme appeal she exerts on masculine men.

The psychological profile of this woman is usually totally different from the LD woman. She is more prone to exhibit *drama* during conflict situations and throughout her relationships with men. What we refer to as "drama" is actually a means by which the cortical part of the brain tries to keep control over limbic system, during episodes of powerful hormonal effects of arousal.

In other words, an HD woman will also face strong internal, moral pressure from her superego — or strong outer pressure from society — in regards to controlling her arousal. When this pressure becomes strong enough, the woman will exhibit drama. Psychologists used to refer to this phenomenon as *hysteria*. The modern term for hysteria is *dissociative behavior*.

It's very interesting to note how nature is working here: weaker men will tend to react to the HD woman's drama by arguing or withdrawing out of fear or fatigue. However, the stronger the man is, the less he will fear the woman's dissociative behavior and the more likely he is to successfully deliver to her some "medicine" that is likely to calm her down: great sex!

In our opinion, the natural purpose of the HD woman's dissociative behavior or drama is to short-circuit male logic so that the male becomes sexually aggressive and more prone to cause a pregnancy. In fact, female drama is almost unbearable to the male brain and a man will tend do almost anything to get a release from that.

From our point of view, it follows that many home violence cases can be traced back to encounters between an LSE HD woman and an aggressive, LSE Alpha male who is unable to control his aggressive tendencies when faced with feminine drama.

Calibrating Sex Drive

Here is an interesting observation we've made through experience: you can calibrate the woman's drive to your own drive over time. If you want things hotter, run more attraction material when you see her. And then, make sure you can sex her good everytime you see her, and *do not* take the sex for granted.

On the other hand, If you want to lower her sex drive, involve her more often in logical conversation, which will put her cerebral cortex to work, thereby overriding the emotional brain's impetus towards sexual engagement. This is guaranteed to work for all women, except the few who are actually aroused by intellectual conversation![1]

If you are an HD male, it makes sense that if you decide to have

[1]Women's extraordinarily wide range of sexual blueprints again demonstrates nature's strategy of widening the genetic pool.

a particular woman as your primary (or only) sexual partner, that she should also be HD.

If you are more of an LD man, you will also want to choose a partner that is compatible with you in that regard, unless you are completely comfortable with the idea of her getting her needs met elsewhere on occasion. This doesn't necessarily mean structuring a sexually open relationship, but it does mean taking the lead to help her effectively channel her emotional energy for your mutual benefit.

By learning how to calibrate to each woman, you will have a better idea wether you and your partner are sexually compatible. Before we get into details on how to screen a woman for either HD or LD, we need to understand some key differences between the way men and women think and function sexually.

Self-Esteem Considerations

When we consider sex drive alongside the factor of self esteem, we derive additional, different categories of women. Bear in mind that each of these qualities exist on a continuum, and what we are presenting here are archetypes. Calibrate accordingly to the woman or women in your life.

The HSE/HD Woman

This type of woman is the dream of every man but not many men can actually deal with her. She has a very strong sexual drive backed up by a very good self-esteem. She is like a Ferrari with a strong motor and an experienced driver driving it. This type of woman will test her man — from the very beginning — for *leadership* qualities. She will be able to remain a good companion to him for as long as is the alpha in the relationship. One of the most distinctive traits of the HSE woman is the relative absence of self-destructiveness from her personality. However, her high level of energy means that she is not suitable for every man. She can be the ideal woman for men who are exceptionally strong in both mind and body.

The HSE/LD Woman

This is also a very good woman, but certainly not suited as the sole woman for a man who is very HD. This woman's sexuality is meant by nature to be sublimated as much as possible, in order to ensure the care of herself and her children. This is a good woman for a man who is very much into his business and who does not have too much time for romance. But the man should hope that she never meets a man who is able to act on her emotionality. In fact, this type of woman is also programmed to change herself into HD when she meets a man who presents a real mental challenge to her.

The HSE/LD woman could, under certain circumstances, feel very strong sexual attraction for a man who is strictly not in the position of her Provider but in the position of her Lover. Very often, this would be a man who does not live with her on her home territory. A man should always remember that the biological purpose of this woman is not so much the man, but rather the child.

The LSE/HD Woman

You do not want to be this woman's husband or boyfriend, but you can be her Lover so long as you do not share keys to a home with her. This is the kind of woman who often has been verbally or physically abused by several former boyfriends or husbands. With a mere superficial observation she may seem to be the victim, but what happens in real life is that she will tend to test men for the most primitive and low-level Alpha qualities: skills for violence and abuse. Her extremely strong sexual drive is paired with a total lack of control over her emotionality and actions. This is obviously a dangerous woman. Among this group you can find a lot of man-haters, but more often in this group there are a lot of psychologically-disturbed women with a lot of self-destructive tendencies. Here, a strong sexual drive is linked to a feeling of being worthless as human being.

The LSE/LD Woman

You should not be her husband or boyfriend and neither should you be her Lover. This woman is usually continuously depressed. In this group you will find a lot of man-haters and women with Borderline Personality Disorder. What can be extremely dangerous about this type of woman is that she may seem to be, at first glance, a totally normal, shy woman who is kind and affectionate. In reality, behind that facade there is a woman who is used to owning men through the use of suffering and sexual deprivation. Slowly but surely, she brings any man who is with her into total submission, to his material detriment.

Verbal Stimulation

Many women are highly dependent on verbal stimulation to be able to enjoy their sexuality fully. As experienced players we have known for years that one of the main roads to having a woman sexually aroused is through the use of rich, verbal descriptions. Brizendine [7] states:

> "Connecting through talking activates the pleasure centers in a girl's brain. We're not talking about a small amount of pleasure. This is huge. It's a major dopamine and oxytocin rush, which is the biggest, fattest neurological reward you can get outside of an orgasm."

In our experience, female arousal, and the pleasure connected with talking that Brizendine writes about, are actually not separated from each other. Bluntly put, effectively delivering rich, descriptive speech makes women horny.

But there is much more! A woman is dependent upon the actions and the attitude of her man with respect to how aroused she is able to become. That is, a woman is in some ways just like as it is written in the Bible; a part of the man's body. This is because in order for her to be sexually receptive, she first has to find within a man a combination of several attributes. Based on our experience, a combination of male sexual dominance, and the skill of verbally stimulating emotions within a woman, will cause a very large number of women to become irresistibly sexually attracted.

Nature, however, has been cruel. It is not natural for most men to be so verbally descriptive. If a man is too verbally descriptive with a woman on an ongoing basis, this will eventually lead to the emasculation of this man, or the perception that he is a homosexual. In fact, such a man will tend to become more and more submissive as he agrees to verbally and emotionally open himself up to the woman.

When a man becomes more and more effeminate by opening himself up emotionally to a woman, female attraction towards that man will invariably plummet. This is because the relationship is lacking the other important quality that a woman needs for sexual arousal: male dominance. [2]

When a man allows himself to open up to a woman for too long of a time, he is in effect being slowly transformed into a woman, from her point of view. At the very beginning, opening up in this way will create a huge increase in her sexual attraction, but eventually, if the man gives up his masculine dominance in the process, it will cause her to her lose her attraction for him.

Incipient Bisexuality

There is evidence that a man is able to arouse a woman via verbal stimulation due an incipient bisexuality in the female arousal process. Apparently, women can be aroused in two distinct ways:

1. Heterosexually, via male sexual dominance. This happens when men do what is natural to them: act dominant.

[2] Decker Cunov, founder of the Authentic Man Program, has developed a coaching program teaching men to become emotionally open, *while remaining fully masculine.*

2. Bisexually or homosexually, via verbal stimulation. This is inherently a lesbian-type of arousal because the use of verbal, rich descriptions when arousing a female is not natural most to men.

According to Chivers et al. [10], female arousal is stimulated by both men and women:

> "In contrast to men, both heterosexual and lesbian women tend to become sexually aroused by both male and female erotica, and, thus, have a bisexual arousal pattern.... These findings likely represent a fundamental difference between men's and women's brains and have important implications for understanding how sexual orientation development differs between men and women." —J. Michael Bailey, professor and chair of psychology at Northwestern and senior researcher of the study "A Sex Difference in the Specificity of Sexual Arousal."

Practical Advice

It is vitally important to determine whether a woman is LD or HD before deciding whether to enter into a long-term relationship with her, because her behavior and the dynamics of a relationship with her will totally different, depending on her sex drive. We already gave you some guidelines by which to screen for a woman's sex drive in Chapters 9 and 10.

Now, based on your deeper understanding of how and why women become sexually aroused, you have the tools to look deeper. When the topics of sex and sexuality come up in your conversation with a woman — and you have properly screened her as either HSE or LSE — then her reactions to such topics can also help to identify the level of her sex drive.

One huge mistake that men typically make in this area is not recognizing the nature of a woman's tests. If a man is unsure of himself and his sexuality, a woman may in fact feign disinterest in sex, or act as if she is tired or busy, in order to test the man's self-confidence and also to test the man's sex drive. The worst thing you can do is act needy; that is, act as if sex is some sort of a gift that the woman bestows upon you in exchange for acting like a so-called "nice guy," as described in Glover's *No More Mr. Nice Guy* [11]). Needy behavior is often fatal to relationships.

It must also be noted that if you understand all of the concepts of this book and apply them rigorously, your partner's sex drive should be higher during the time she is in a relationship with you than it would be otherwise. When you are sexually attracted to someone it is natural that your desire for sex would increase, either somewhat or a lot.

Instead of viewing sex as a woman's gift to you, be a leader: someone who bestows sexual pleasure upon the woman and takes it for himself. If you know within yourself that you can bring a particular woman to orgasm, and you have identified the nature of her testing (HSE or LSE), then you can easily compare the level of her sex drive to yours.

Develop Masculine Sexual Leadership

One of the keys to great sexuality in a man is being able to master two seemingly-contradictory states of mind within yourself. For one, you need to be fully conscious of the signals the woman's body and mind are giving off, in order to calibrate your movements and pace. On the other hand, acting like a subservient wussy, who is only concerned with the woman's pleasure and ignorant of his own body, is a sexual turnoff to most women. Therefore, what you need in the bedroom, as anywhere else in life, are the qualities of a leader. A leader in this context is someone who is aware of his own body and his own pleasure — and he will take what he wants when he wants it — but at the same time he is sensitive to the needs of his partner, who also has a need to be pleased.

Once you have the experience and understanding to really, really please any woman both mentally and sexually, it will be much easier to gauge how much of a sex drive any particular woman has. You'll be able to quickly ascertain how often a specific woman wants to come back for more in relation to how often you want sex. Even better, you will be able to quickly screen for a woman with whom you are most sexually compatible with before committing to a long-term relationship.

15 Last Minute Resistance

Stop right there!
I gotta know right now
Before we go any further
Do you love me?
Will you love me forever?
Do you need me?
— *Paradise by the Dashboard Light*, by Meatloaf

HAVE you ever been with a woman and having a great time as things progressed to physical play? Maybe things got started with a dance to a favorite song, and then, slowly but surely, your bodies became closer and closer as your arousal increased. You could feel her arousal increasing too, as her kisses became more passionate and she began to pull your body closer to hers. At some point, one of you made a decision to get yourselves into more private surroundings, and the kisses and the touching continued to escalate. You and your woman were connecting on every level, and you became certain within yourself that the connection the two of you were experiencing could not be more perfect. And then, suddenly, she pulled back and said, "Stop!"

If you are like most men, at one time or another you have experienced something similar to the scenario we just described. And, like most men, you were probably left scratching your head wondering "what went wrong?." Actually, nothing went wrong, the woman is responding appropriately. This phenomenon is known as Last-Minute Resistance (LMR) and virtually every man has experienced it. LMR can be defined as female resistance to sexual intercourse, *after* the female has already agreed to spend time in an isolated venue with a man.

Intelligent men who have agonized over this phenomenon have come up with technology that allows one to effectively deal with LMR, while at the same time allowing the woman to maintain her self-respect. Later in the chapter, we will provide you with the specific tactics that every man would love to have with respect to LMR. But first, let's make a detailed examination of the evolutionary underpinnings of LMR.

LMR has been described by women as a horrible, fearful emotion that envelops them at a particular threshold. The threshold varies among women. One woman may draw the line at removing her jeans, another at removing her panties. The same woman may have a different threshold depending on the man, or the environment of the encounter, or both. A few women have very little LMR.

One of the reasons that LMR can be so frustrating for the man involved is that this reaction often occurs right at the point of no return of the sexual encounter; the point where a woman realizes that if she goes one step further, she is going to end up having sex with the man she is with. To put it simply, this fear comes down to a fundamental question that the woman *feels* inside: "should I — or should I not — have sex with this man (yet)?" Every single woman on the planet will feel this emotion at one time or another in her life, and to varying degrees.

LMR is difficult for men to understand, because men do not experience this in the same way. Men do have a corresponding fear, one that is experienced at the very beginning of the sexual encounter, and that is the fear of the approach. Since women do not normally approach men, they often find it difficult to understand this male fear, in the same way men find it hard to understand LMR.

LMR is a mechanism that is hardwired into the biology of virtually every woman on the planet, no matter what her level of sexual experience or her cultural background. In biological terms, LMR serves two purposes in benefit of the woman.

Biological and Sociological Purposes of LMR

If a woman becomes impregnated by a man and the man does not stick around to protect her and her child, this can be a real danger for the woman. This is a basic, instinctual fear inside almost every woman alive. The fear persists in spite of the fact that today's society allows women the freedom to choose one man for pregnancy, another man to support her, and other men for fun on the side. Today, health care for most women is far superior to the days when pregnancy meant death for 50 per cent or more of childbearing women. In those days, being abandoned by her mate could mean ostracism, poverty and even death for a woman. Today, the state will give a woman full custody of her children, order that child support be paid, and remove most of the harsh consequences of pregnancy, but these are recent societal developments which do not alter a woman's biological makeup.

LMR is also an instinctual reaction from females induced when she finds herself in a state of isolation. We believe this reaction fulfills two roles: it is designed to maximize her evolutionary value, and to preserve her physical safety. In our culture, a woman's being isolated with a male has a sexual meaning. A lot of cultural norms and institutions have been put in place with the sole purpose of prohibiting females from being in a state of isolation with a man to whom she is not married. Physical safety considerations come from both the biological risk of childbirth, which is dangerous for women, and getting caught in a "compromising" situation has far more lethal ramifications on the African savannah where humans first evolved.

Usually, a man who is directing his efforts towards having sex with a woman will attempt to get the woman into a state of isolation in order to achieve his goal. Men in particular hold the viewpoint that if a female agrees to isolation with a male, she is desiring to have intercourse with him. However, that is not necessarily the case.

Basically, when a female has agreed to be in an isolated venue with a man, she has decided (at least subconsciously) that the male in question is superior in terms of genetic fitness, in comparison to all the other males in her proximity. At a minimum, she would like for others observing the interaction to *believe* that she feels this way about the man. Since LMR means frustration for the man and puts him in a position of *wanting something* from the female, exhibiting LMR gives her some power over him. In this way, she can maximize her potential control over him.

It is therefore important to detect the *underlying meaning* of the LMR being displayed.

Two types of LMR

If a woman has LMR out of an inability to be sexually receptive to a man, or because of difficulties in accepting *any* man as sexual human being, then what we have is LSE LMR, which is a pathological form of LMR.

If a woman has LMR for a biological and evolutionary need to test her male's psychological strength and control over his instincts — in other words, to test for his lack of neediness — then we have HSE LMR.

HSE LMR is a trademark of a female who is a very strong individual in terms of her rational control over her biological instincts. Such a woman wants to be sure to choose only strong males as her sexual partner. A "strong male" in this context is one who does not *need* her, either sexually or psychologically.

These are of course general descriptions; most women will have a mixture of both HSE and LSE. When you properly screen a woman for her self esteem, then you will be able to avoid the pain and frustration that comes from dealing with a woman with LSE LMR. You can rest assured that a woman who would exhibit LSE LMR with you at the beginning of your relationship will consistently do so, as long as your relationship with her lasts. She will do so because he has indicated from the out-set that this type of behavior is either acceptable or tolerable to him.

Dealing with LMR

It should now be obvious to you, the reader, that you will want to avoid women who exhibit LSE LMR. A relationship with a woman like that will constantly put you in the position of a man who is made to feel like his natural male desires are somehow wrong or immoral, and at a minimum, a burden to the woman he is with. In reality, for a sexual relationship to function in a healthy way, you should view sex as *your* gift to *her. The gift a woman gives you is her love, not her sex.*

That being said, there remains the issue of legitimate, HSE LMR, where a woman is merely testing you for strength because of her own high self-esteem. As we mentioned in the last paragraph, the way to pass that test is to demonstrate that you do not need her, either sexually or psychologically. Demonstrating this positions you as a man of strength.

Let's say for example that you are about to reach the point of no return, and your woman abruptly says "we should stop." The correct procedure here is not to get upset or angry, or to sulk or complain. Rather, you will want to demonstrate that you understand this phenomenon, which implies that you've seen it before, and that you are not at all troubled by it. Remember, sex is a gift from you to her. If you decide that you no longer feel like cuddling with her, then you can get up and make a sandwich, go for a walk, or check your email. Remember, it is *absolutely vital* that the woman not feel that she has been able to upset you by this course of events.

Preempting LMR

If you are dealing with a sexually healthy, HSE woman, remember that her LMR reaction is a test for her to judge your strength and your dependence on her. Before mating, a woman needs to feel like she is with a man who is strong and able to take care of her and her child in a case of pregnancy. If a man demonstrates that he is dependent on her for either sex or psychological support, she instinctively knows that he is not the man with the best genes for her. And the best way to judge a man's strength is to observe him under pressure. These tests are merely part of the female biological instinct.

Women also have an instinctual fear of being abandoned by a

man who, while he may be very attractive to her in terms of his strength, may not be willing to stick around long enough to ensure the safety of her and her child.

When couples fall in love, there is a chemical process that occurs the brain known as *pair bonding*. The biological purpose of pair bonding is to ensure that a couple stays together long enough in order to ensure the survival of both the mother and the child.

One way to preempt the naturally occurring LMR in a healthy, HSE woman is to encourage pair bonding throughout the courtship process. Assure her with words such as: "I feel that you and I have a really special connection," or "Even though we are here amongst all of our friends and loved ones, my mind is on you all the time." These words are effective, with the following caveats. Such statements should never be made in an approval-seeking way, and should only be done in the context of building comfort with a woman who is obviously already attracted to you. *And it should go without saying that that if you do not feel pair bonded with her, don't manipulate her emotions by telling her you do.*

The Rapo Game

Every once in a while, a woman will come along and give you all the right signals, all the way up until it's time to lift her skirt. Then, she not only balks at your advances, but becomes indignant about the entire notion of sexual intimacy. In other words, she tricks you. The best description of this phenomenon is Eric Berne's "Rapo Game" [12]. If you meet a woman like this, your absolute best bet is to project both strength and absolute disinterest. Showing any weakness, such as when apologizing or supplicating may induce a further attack, with possible adverse legal consequences. Disinterest means exactly that: you *never* want to make an overture of any sort towards this type of a woman. And best to never be isolated with her either.

For whatever reason, you may be required to interact with such a woman in a social context, and you may be in a position where you must always respond to her in a pleasant and polite manner. Such women know that they hold *all* the cards, and that society will completely back them and any allegations they make. The game for these women is the obtaining of male attention, but in a very sick way. If you can avoid giving such women your attention, you will go a long way towards defusing future problems for yourself.

16 The Madonna/whore Complex

And the angel said unto her,
"Fear not, Mary: for thou hast found favour with God."
— Luke 1:30, *King James Bible*

THE Madonna/whore Complex is a widespread phenomenon of modern life. We can properly call it a meme, or a mind virus, that affects the majority of people today, both men and women. The presence of this meme directly contributes to sexual frustration in both men and women, with men relegated to consuming pornography, and women consuming romance novels, both in astonishing quantities. Both the pornography and romance novel industries are worth billions of dollars every single year.

In spite of that, most men will not openly admit to being regular consumers of pornography. Most women will blush and deny if asked about their propensity towards romance novels. Sexual satisfaction for many, if not most people, comes via secret fantasy worlds. Men and women both spend lots of time fantasizing about other people having hot sex and living out exciting romantic lives.

Nowadays, women even try to match male behavior by going to watch male strippers and being more proactive about suggesting sex . When that type of female assertiveness is not an expression of free will, it actually derives itself from the complex, too.

We believe that one of the primary causes of this secret sexual life, and the inability of many people to create real, exciting and passionate relationships with other human beings that they can touch, feel and interact with, is the Madonna/whore Complex.

One of the most deleterious effects of the Madonna/whore complex in our society is that there is a psychological tendency to deny or ignore the existance of female sexual arousal. Because of this, many people do not realize that female sexual desire is a phenomenon that can be detected — not only by studying the female orgasm — but also by studying the female's:

1. Verbal Expression (female language and its relationship to the level of her arousal.)

2. Behavior (the relationship between a female's manifested behavior and her level of arousal.)

3. Facial Expression and Body Language (the non-verbal expression of female arousal.)

In the mind of the average guy, there is a total black hole in this area. Many men tend to view women as merely a "walking vagina." Some men have some knowledge about the female orgasm and yet absolutely no knowledge of how a woman's sexual desire affects her behavior and her verbal and non-verbal expression. And too many men, sad to say, have absolutely no knowledge about the female orgasm and how it relates to her personality.

What is the Madonna/whore Complex?

There does not appear to be a single, universally-accepted definition of the Madonna/whore Complex. According to one definition we like,[1], the Madonna/whore Complex refers to a phenomenon where men view their mates as sacred love objects, too pure to be sullied with the ugliness of sexual interaction, like a Madonna.

Women who engage in raw and passionate sex, such as the women of pornography, are considered "whores" or even worse. These women are secretly admired from afar, through the pages of a magazine or on the television screen, but they are never loved openly and directly.

Freud wrote that the Complex arises in a man as a result of very close bonding with his mother, which the man never truly outgrows. The man seeks out a wife to replace the lost bonding with his mother, and because having sex with his mother

[1] http://en.wikipedia.org/wiki/Madonna-whore_complex

would be incest, he becomes subconsciously repelled from his wife in a sexual way.

An alternative explanation comes from Primal Theory, which posits that the complex results from a cold and distant mother; a mother who has not met the male child's need for affectionate intimacy. Either way, such a man may seek out and marry a supposedly "pure" woman to love, treasure, and protect. But in his mind, this is not a woman with whom one would have dirty, nasty sex.

The existence of the complex is not disputed. It is in fact very real, and most everyone has an intuitive understanding of what it means for them personally.

A dissociation between "sex" and "love" is omnipresent in our culture, even in our English language. For example, a man under the effect of the Complex may define the sexual activity a woman has with other men as "sex", and the sexual activity she has with him as "love". A woman, on the other hand, can define making love with her husband as "dirty sex", but when she falls in love in a romantic way with a lover in an extra-marital affair she may define it as "making love with my lover".

This conflict is spread throughout our culture. Both men and women alike love the idea of raw, passionate sex. Yet, most men walk through life being afraid of women and treating them like Madonnas. The modern man often has a secret, vicarious relationship with the whores of pornography, and a timid, asexual relationship with all other women, including his intimate partners.

Where does it come from?

Men have learned since childhood that the *Mother* is a sacred creature, and our culture and the powerful messages it conveys through television and other media teaches that women are to be viewed as either good or bad, depending largely on their ability to suppress their sexuality and display mother-like qualities of compassion and nurturing.

The woman who has a strong sexuality and a free life, is, in the minds of many men, the Whore. The woman who gives birth to them, takes care of them and is close to them in their moments of despair is the Madonna.

When a man suffers from the Complex and finds himself in a relationship, confusion often arises as to which category he should place his girlfriend or wife. Many men fantasize about a woman that is wild in bed, but if they picture their wives like that then they start to feel jealousy. If their woman is active in bed and seems to enjoy sex "too much", the man may even start to feel a certain dislike towards her, feeling that she is too "slutty" to be a "good" wife.

Many men suffer because they automatically place their girlfriends or wives into the Madonna category, but they still secretly long for sex with a whore. In this case the woman may suffer from a great deal of sexual frustration, and she may adopt her man's view that too much enjoyment of sex by a woman is *shameful*. In this case she will gradually lose her ability to be sexually uninhibited with her man and begin to avoid sex with him. The men will then often complain that their "good" girlfriend no longer wants to make love, and they will be astonished when she decides to seek out another sexual partner, one who *understands* her needs as a woman.

But what, exactly, causes this Complex? Is it possible to enjoy a rich and deep relationship with a woman who is a freak in the sack? For the average guy, it's hard to know which category to place the woman in front of him. To be totally frank, most women are aware of this conflict within men and will sometimes intentionally play this dual card of being either a Madonna or a whore. It is to the woman's advantage to have you invest mental energy into her in this way. Before we give you the solution to this dilemma, we'll provide some further detail about why women act the way that they do.

Many of us were taught by our mothers especially that sex is something to be hidden, kept secret and often that it is something shameful. We are especially fed the cultural message that it's ok for boys to brag in the locker room about sexual exploits, many of which never even happened or are exaggerated. A young woman who is the subject of such tales can often face the ridicule and scorn of her peers. In ancient times and still today in more traditional countries, a woman can be put to death on the suspicion of committing illicit sexual acts. Although attitudes have relaxed quite a bit in the past few decades, women who are promiscuous are generally not viewed in the same favorable light that promiscuous men are.

To put it another way, both girls and boys are taught from a very young age that good girls are not free to enjoy sex in the same way that boys are. Girls who enjoy sex too much or who are too open and direct with their sexuality are called horrible names and punished within their social group, or worse, cast out completely.

Do I have the Complex?

If you possess a belief that good girls do not enjoy sex in the same way that "bad" girls do, you have the Complex. If you are afraid to be sexually agressive with your wife or girlfriend, and yet masturbate regularly to pornography, then you probably also have this complex. If you find yourself repeating and laughing at common jokes such as "all men are pigs," or "he can't help it, he's a guy," then that would be another indication. If you regularly engage in wussy, tip-toe-on-eggshells type behavior around women that you are sexually attracted to, then you definitely need to work on this issue.

Understand that to truly be liberated from the Complex, your internal attitudes and views about women and female sexuality will need a radical makeover.

How can a Man Avoid Being Harmed by this Phenomenon?

What is really astonishing about the existence of the Complex is the fact that women enjoy sex *as much* and *often more* than men do. One only needs to take a look at a typical romance novel, or some female-authored erotica like Nancy Friday's *My Secret Garden*, to realize that women have wonderfully explicit sexual imaginations and desires.

As a mature adult male, you should recognize that it is a beautiful and healthy thing for a woman to have a strong and wild sex drive. The sex drive of a woman says little about her character or her personality, other than her appetite for sex. In Chapter 7 on Female Archetypes we dealt in depth with the personality types of women. As you should well understand by now, many good women have an extremely high sex drive, and there are also dangerous women to be avoided that do not possess a high sex drive. It is good for a man to appreciate the indisputable truth that sex for a woman is a beautiful, natural expression of her femininity and that it should be encouraged and praised, never condemned or feared.

Love a Woman for Who She Is

"Unconditional love" is when you love a woman for who and what she *is* and not for who you think she *should be*. When a man is forced by circumstances to give a woman *conditional* love he feels bad inside. Unfortunately, men do not talk about this sort of thing with each other. Men will rarely admit it, but when they really love a woman they do it with every breath, and with every cell of their body and mind. This is one of the lesser-known reasons that men are always trying to hide their feelings in favor of their mission. They persistently try to keep themselves "tough" and shut off from the *emotional* world. Men also have many other reasons for suppressing emotions, but love for a woman is the most sensitive reason.

When is a man forced to give conditional love to a woman? He becomes obliged to do so when he is put in a situation where he has to choose between his honor, his self respect, and his vital interests on the one hand — and giving his love to the woman on the other hand. The experience of being forced to stop giving love to his woman and to the members of his intimate group is the one of the most deleterious and dangerous experiences a man can face in his life.

For a man, having to withdraw his love is especially painful, because to maintain his manhood he has to take the responsibility of repressing the love he naturally feels within himself, if circumstances oblige him to do so. A masculine man is in fact totally dominated by the instinct of being the protector of women and children. The experience of loving them and protecting them is — by instinct — extremely important to him.

As men of honor, we personally do not consider "real men" those who try to escape their natural role as the Alpha of their group.

If one wanted to efficiently and completely destroy a man emotionally, then one would merely need to demonstrate to him in a clear way that he is *useless* as a protector to the members of his group; to other men, to his women and to his children.

Men are tough: they have been trained throughout history to do what must be done. A man's mission is his honor. If a real man is put to choose between his honor, his mission and the woman he loves he will choose his honor and his mission. And his woman — if she is a real woman — will love him for that.

If a real man is put to choose between his honor and love he will choose honor. He will suffer, but he will do so. If a man gives up his honor and his mission for his woman, then his woman may pretend to love him but her love for him will be already dead in her heart.

As Franco often says, being a man can be a lonely business.

Next, we'll show how your knowledge of the Complex actually puts you at a distinct advantage over the vast majority of men when it comes to dealing with women.

17 Dealing with the Madonna/whore Complex

I'm just a bad girl, that's why we get along
Won't make excuses for anything I'm doing wrong
I'll pull the trigger in a flash
Watch out honey, step back
(Oooh) What's the use in playing it safe?
(Oooh) Wouldn't you rather misbehave?
— *Dirty Laundry*, by BitterSweet

By recognizing the true nature of women as passionate sexual creatures, and by eliminating from your mind the completely *false choice* that says a woman must either be a whore or a Madonna, you put yourself at a huge advantage over most men today. Because so few men really understand the Madonna/whore complex, you will soon discover that there is a whole world of women that are frustrated and lonely and looking for sexual adventures.

In order for her to truly express herself sexually, a woman needs to *feel* that the man she chooses to be with will not expose her to ridicule. She must be confident that he will not embarrass her in public or in front of her friends and family. Even more fearful for a woman is the prospect of being considered trash by the very man that she has chosen to give herself to sexually.

One of the crucial keys to having a lot of women feeling sexually comfortable with you as a man is to eliminate any traces of the Complex in your mind and attitude. What are some of the ways that you can let a woman know that you've completely eliminated the Complex from your life?

There are several things a man must do to relax the boundaries that society and he himself may be imposing on his sexual life. First, understand the traditional female response to the Complex, which is known as the Anti-Slut Defense (ASD). In the next chapter, we go into detail with regards to ASD and provide you with the tools you need to overcome it.

The next thing you need to do in relation to the Complex is to thoroughly examine your own belief system. Be honest with yourself and see whether you have any presence of the Complex within you. Then make a sincere and determined effort to get a deep understanding of how it has been affecting you and your views towards women.

Finally, subcommunicate to your lover or mate that wild sexual adventure is normal and healthy, even though you understand that it's still important in our society to be very discreet about such beliefs and behavior. Let's examine each of these points in more detail.

Understand Yourself

All of us have some aspect of the Complex. From the perspective of Evolutionary Psychology, the Complex may also serve to distinguish in both men and women such roles as the *Lover* versus the *Provider.* If you are currently in a loving relationship with a woman, consider the case where she reveals that she has always had a powerful fantasy of being penetrated by two men at once. How would you feel about this? Suppose you are deeply in love with this women. Does this revelation change your feelings for her? Would you be willing to allow her to explore this fantasy, or would you feel betrayed by her admission? Here is the social reality: most women have outrageous fantasies, while most men are completely, totally, and irrevocably unable to emotionally handle such rampant female sexuality.

But let's say that, unlike most men, you wish to freely enjoy women in both aspects, Madonna and whore. In that case, you will need to rewire both yourself and your relationship in the following ways:

- First, make sure you are completely comfortable with the Madonna side of your relationship. This could take some work if you are currently in a rocky relationship, and you will need the baseline of trust and comfort. There are times when a woman wants to be motherly and feel like a lady. This does not mean that you will forfeit your leadership role in the relationship. However, there are times when a woman can properly enjoy taking care of her man and expressing tenderness and affection towards him. More on this point is covered in Chapter 19, "Male Qualities Attractive to Women".

- Become comfortable with *your own* sexual needs and desires. If you are uncomfortable with your very real desire to do X, Y or Z with some "slut" it is 100% certain your woman will feel uncomfortable with the idea as well. This may take some profound personal reevaluation.

- Understand your personal boundaries. Write them out if necessary. Be detailed and very specific. Imagine situations that "couldn't possibly happen."

- Start subcommunicating that you are comfortable with sexually expressive women. That "sluttinesss" is a sexually attractive quality. This is easy when it's true.

- Lose your ego. It is very likely that your woman fantasizes about other men once in a while. Possibly even when you are sexually engaged. That is, while you are pretending she is Pamela Andersen, she may be pretending you are Jude Law (or whomever). It's normal. Deal with it. Play with it even, if you're man enough.

- Establish a deep, intimate, loving connection with her such that your interactions with her are appreciative. That is, you are not giving with the expectation of being repaid by her, but rather, you are giving to her out of appreciation. Once you are able to truly appreciate a woman as an intensely sexual being, she will feel much more comfortable deeply opening herself up to you. And you will feel comfortable with the responsibility that such trust entails.

- Make sure that your normal sexual relations with the woman are otherwise outstanding. Make sure she is thoroughly and properly well-sexed.

- At this point, sexual experimentation is almost a given. She will want to be sexually experimental with you!

If at any point during this process, your woman feels any judgement about her sexuality from you, or feels any social pressure from friends or family, it's game over. At least temporarily. For this reason, the quality of discretion is also very important. For more information on how to use discretion in your dealings with women, please see Chapter 5 on female subcommunication and Chapter 18 on the Anti-Slut Defense.

Have a Realistic View of the Woman

The best way to avoid the deleterious influence of the Complex is to have enough real-life experience with women. Young men should avoid committed relationships with women if they do not first have more casual relationships with women, especially if they come from a cultural background where the Complex is very much present, such as North America. If you believe in marriage and want to marry that one special woman you meet while you are still young, then it is absolutely crucial that you pay attention to female psychology and that you dedicate your-self to the understanding of the female psyche and a woman's emotional life.

If you get into a relationship with a woman, without first having a realistic view of what it actually *means* to be a woman — including all of the psychological and cultural forces at work that we've discussed here — then be assured that you are going to face a lot of trouble and disappointment. A realistic view of women starts with the acceptance that they are sexual human beings with healthy sexual desires. The cultural influences that we've been bombarded with since childhood regarding Madonnas and whores does not reflect reality. The Madonna/whore complex is in fact an extremely sick, dissociative distortion of reality.

The Female View of Sex and Politics

Another factor which makes this even more complicated is the fact that the Complex has very much to do with gender politics and the balance of power between men and women. One woman under the effect of the Complex can create for herself a life where her sexuality has been totally taken out of the equation when it comes to her relationships with men. A different woman may be able to remove the "Madonna" part from her life completely and effectively use her sexuality as a means to achieve social power.

For example, the woman who sacrifices herself and her relationships in favor of her secular career is actually under the effect of the Complex. The woman who deliberately suppresses all of her natural needs for emotional connection and love, and who uses sex as a means to achieve power over men, is also under the effect of the Complex, but for different reasons.

Case Study: The Pastor

One recent case in the US news involves Ted Haggard, a prominent pastor of a large Evangelical denomination. For whatever reason, conjugal relations with his wife did not provide enough sexual fulfillment for him, leading our unfortunate pastor into the realm of hot, gay, tweaker sex. This cost him his job of course, once he got busted. Although many facts of the case are not at all clear, it is self-evident that Mr Haggard was not sexually satisfied within the constraints of his marriage.

Individual psychology is very complex and in the case in question, issues connected with both the inner psychological world as well as issues connected with interpersonal relationships are likely to be involved. Although we cannot say for certain, Mr. Haggard is congruent with the Madonna/whore Complex. We can also see evidence of the Complex in society's reaction to this case. The magnitude of the public reaction demonstrates just how deeply this Complex is ingrained in our society.

One of the aims of this book is to educate men, so that they can have a more relaxed and realistic view of female sexuality. We believe that many of these types of problems could be avoided, if men and women could learn to meet each other's sexual needs without having to psychologically dissociate from each other, and without this compulsion to divide women into two pieces in a schizophrenic way. While homosexuality is very-well accepted in many civilized countries, a single honorable man's entire life's work may be permanently damaged by his psychological dissociation of sexuality. It is obvious that this dissociation of sexuality that is caused by the Complex is very harmful and is the cause of such a huge collective reaction of denial. In this case there is evidence of a psychotic *group* reaction coming from within the pastor's religious social network.

Case Study: The Sports Celebrity

In another case, O.J. Simpson, a famous sports celebrity, had been accused of the murder of his own wife and her lover. Evidence about his terrible jealousy towards her and his abusive behavior have been widely reported in the media. The existence of the Madonna/whore Complex is in this case evident. It seems that Mr. Simpson was regularly cheating on his wife, while at the same time jealously accusing her of the very same act. He apparently could not accept the fact that she is a whole woman, and that the jealousy within him reflects a denial of his woman's sexual desire. Mr. Simpson was acquitted of all the criminal charges against him, but he did in fact come dangerously close to the electric chair. Mr. Simpson's reaction toward his wife can be considered to be a *focused* psychotic reaction, in that it is manifested specifically towards one situation and one person. At the root of such a psychotic reaction is once again the Madonna/whore Complex.

Case Study: The Prince

In another country, Prince Charles of Wales and his relationship to a very wild, adventurous woman named Lady Diana Spencer was regularly reported on in the media. The wife of the Prince, Ms. Spencer, now deceased, was what we would define as an LSE Adventuress type of woman. She had suffered from bulimia and from personal identity problems and from depression. In spite of these LSE traits, Ms. Spencer was a great woman, dedicated to children and to many charitable works.

As far as we can surmise, Prince Charles too is a great man who is devoted to his country. However, he faced a recurring problem with his former wife. We can make an educated guess that he was probably too much of a "Nice Guy" for a woman like Lady Diana. A Nice Guy is someone who is not able to recognize an Adventuress for who she is: a woman who has possibly suffered from neglect in her childhood, who is often in constant need of attention, and usually craves a high degree of external stimulation in one form or another. The Nice Guy will quite often and quite easily commit the terrible mistake of trying to "fix her" or "improve her."

For a woman of the Adventuress type, *attention* and *validation* are of paramount concern in her life, and her sexuality is often deeply connected with those needs. It is important to note how Diana's sexuality seemed to flourish as soon as she found another man who is what we would call a "tough guy" or a "bad boy." It was widely reported that she appeared quite happy for the first time in many years. Still, she continued to live a self-destructive life. The story ends with her tragic death in a car accident in Paris, a death whose circumstances are still unclear.

What if Prince Charles would have been able to deal with Ms. Spencer more effectively? Would she still be alive? It is possible that a whole web of psychotic reactions had been caused as a result of the Prince's inability to acknowledge or properly handle the free-mindedness of his wife, triggering a long and complex chain of events which eventually led to her death.

18 The Anti-Slut Defense

What kind of a girl would do
the things you're askin' me to without wedding rings?
Is it what you must do to prove you're a man?
What kind of a girl do you think I am?
— *What Kind of a Girl,* by Loretta Lynn

OFTEN a woman will want to have sex with a man, sometimes very urgently, but she will impose logical reasons, excuses, and other obstacles in order to hinder sex from happening. Especially when a woman is in the presence of her peers or family will she tend to avoid any appearance of promiscuity or of being too readily available for sex. Her corresponding behavior in such situations is referred to as the "Anti-Slut Defense" (ASD).

An experienced man can deflect ASD so as to extract from his woman the best of her sexuality. On the other hand, learning to detect ASD is also important in order for you to be able to determine which woman or women to spend your time and energy on. You should be aware that there is a *socially-induced* ASD, which is present in every woman, and also a *pathological* ASD, which is a sign of a woman who will never be able to fully enjoy her sexuality, even within the boundaries of a socially-acceptable relationship such as marriage. A woman who exhibits strong ASD at all times no matter what the circumstances can surely be considered LSE.

This chapter includes some of the most important material in this book. Your ability to defuse ASD is one of the most powerful weapons you will have for being in a position to sexually satisfy women.

ASD in Seduction

Seducing is the act of first creating attraction within a woman, and soon thereafter a *willingness* to have sex with you. In most cases, you can view the presence of at least *some* of the signs of ASD as a positive thing. Generally speaking, ASD is a sign that you are succeeding in making a woman horny. With your help, a psychologically healthy woman will eventually be able to overcome her ASD and enjoy sex with you.

ASD can be detected by observing a complex of verbal and non-verbal, behavioral responses within the woman. Detecting ASD is not always easy; in fact, the woman will not usually communicate it directly but, rather, she will subcommunicate it.

During the seduction process, you will need to perform an independent interpretation of the woman's subcommunication without actually talking or arguing with her about it. Quite often, the presence of ASD is completely unconscious to the woman. Even in cases where a woman recognizes certain symptoms of ASD within herself, she will rarely discuss this openly with you.

ASD can be noticed when a woman shows signs of general *uneasiness* in conjunction with an increase in her arousal. This is different than when a woman is *testing* you. Usually, a woman tests a man so that she can determine whether or not he is worthy of having sex with her. With ASD, on the other hand, she is already craving sexual relations with you, but she is feeling a sense of inner conflict about her arousal. She may wonder whether she is a slut or a bad woman for being so aroused so quickly in your presence. As was already mentioned, these feelings maybe (somewhat) unconscious and be manifested by a general feeling of discomfort.

Keep in mind that ASD can be very specific: some women may feel like sluts if they have sex with you on the beach and yet be perfectly at ease having sex with you in hotels. Other women may feel that they are sluts if they have sex with you in a hotel and be perfectly at ease on the beach.

A woman's ASD will often be totally illogical and unrelated to the context and situation. For example Franco remembers one of his lovers, a married woman, who felt she was perfectly okay making love with him at her professional studio, and yet she would feel like a slut when presented with the opportunity for a rendezvous at a hotel.

Usually, a woman's feelings of ASD will be projected onto the man in question, meaning that she will tend to feel that it is entirely your fault if she begins to feel badly about feeling slutty.

What is a "Slut", anyway?

When we think in terms of evolutionary advantage, people will tend to label women as "sluts" when they seem to be ignoring certain rules for fair competition among women. Women are always after the highest-value males, and a slut is a woman who is accused of selling her reproductive rights to men at too-low of a price. Women are very competitive in nature and will sometimes enforce the rules of competition through selective labeling of their competitors.

The term "slut" also comes from a perspective of negative moral judgement on the part men with the Madonna/whore complex. These men are in fact scared of competition with other men, and so they label women whom they consider to be "easy" as sluts. A man speaking in such a derogatory fashion about a woman is in fact demonstrating fear of the woman's sexuality and an inability to handle it in a mature fashion.[1]

ASD in Long-Term Relationships

ASD is also rampant in long-term relationships! In fact, it's almost certainly *more* present in long-term relationships with Provider-type men than it is in short term or ephemeral relationships with Lovers.

Think about it from the woman's point of view. She may enjoy a surprisingly wide variety of sexual activity, but her need for personal security and security for her children preclude such activities, when her man is not comfortable with sexually-

[1]"Slut" is a label also applied by men to women who refuse to grant sexual access to such men, while publicly granting access to other males. In this situation, the epithet comes from envy.

engaged women. Suppose he sees on TV or a movie a scene depicting a sexually active woman and exclaims "What a slut she is!" using a tone laden with condemnation or contempt. His judgement on that woman sends powerful messages to the woman he is with, such as:

- He is not comfortable with female sexuality
- He may be supplicating to obtain his woman's approval, saying what he believes she wants to hear
- He does not have very much sexual experience with women. Men with a lot of sexual experience with women know that women as a group enjoy an extremely wide variety of sexual activity.

Women will test for your views on "sluttiness" within a relationship, by making remarks like "Oh that woman is such a slut!" If you are a man who enjoys the company of women, step up and say so: "I know! That's what I like about her so much!" This test is commonly employed early on in a relationship. The woman will use bad-behaving celebrities — or other women she doesn't know personally making similar news — as examples for such comments.

One thing is for sure: if you don't believe a woman is capable of acting in some particular sexual manner, you can be absolutely sure she *won't* act in this way, with you. If such an activity is something she craves, some integral part of her love map, she may find it elsewhere. If you don't take steps to lead her where you want to go, you will never find out one way or another whether she is willing to follow you there. Don't sell her short!

Practical Advice

In our society, it may not be possible to eliminate the phenomenon of ASD entirely, but we can certainly mitigate the incidence and severity of it with the women we choose to interact with. One important way that we can do this is by mastering something known as *Discretion*.

Discretion is the quality that we display as a signal to the woman that we are aware of the prevalence in society of the Madonna/whore complex, and that we have personally dealt with it. We realize that the complex presents a real danger for women in our world; at the very least, she senses danger from it in her subconscious mind. How do you subcommunicate to a woman that she is safe being sexual with you?

Consider when you are in a group of people, and some of the men begin making distasteful comments about a certain woman's sexuality. Are you eager to make fun at the woman's expense? Or consider if you have an opportunity for a secret rendezvous with an attractive woman. Are you the type of person to openly discuss the possibilities with your friends, as if you were a child about to travel to Disney World for the first time? Or would you likely brag about your conquest after the fact to anyone who will listen? Doing any of these things will position you as a man that is not discreet and who cannot be trusted with any decent woman's honor. You will automatically and unfailingly raise the ASD of the women around you. This is something, however, that women will rarely, if ever, talk about. Women simply avoid men who are not discreet.

Men who are enjoying many sexual partners do not need to brag about their conquests as if they somehow "got lucky." Men who want to enjoy the company of many women must first learn to cultivate and display the quality of discretion. You are a man that is comfortable with women and their sexuality, and at the same time you know when to keep your mouth shut. You are not disturbed by female sexual expression and at the same time you know how to discreetly create the circumstances that will allow the woman the freedom to express herself. While you love and enjoy sex and have no embarrassment about your sexual desires as a healthy man, sex is not something so rare and unusual for you that you are compelled to reveal private details to the woman's friends, or even your own friends.

You will find that even women who have a liberated view of sexuality will in fact avoid men who do not display discretion. While many people today will not judge a woman for being promiscuous, other people will still judge her quite harshly. Naturally, she will feel comfortable with non-judgmental people and will want to avoid people with a deeply-ingrained Madonna/whore complex.

Demonstrate Discretion

It's not enough to subcommunicate discretion. You must demonstrate discretion as well. Men who are showoffs, braggarts and boasters, who must have the last word, who crave being the "most in the know," who are addicted to playing "one-up," these men will find demonstrating discretion much more difficult.

Here's how it works: Discussing real sexuality is more or less taboo in nearly all segments of society. When sexuality is discussed, uncomfortable topics often arise quickly, increasing the social and sexual tension. This tension is *invariably* reduced with ridicule. Which is exactly what triggers ASD.

Suppose you and your woman get up to some naughty stuff, stuff that drives her crazy, but she would be mortified if people found out. Now you are both surprised to find that the topic comes up in public discussion, in one of two ways:

1. As innuendo. This is easy: let it pass. If other people in the conversation don't know otherwise, just let them think you're a bit "dull" in such matters and not so quick on the uptake about the sex thing. Your woman will instantly understand and appreciate your actions here.

2. Directly. A little bit tougher: go with the crowd here, and subcommunicate to your woman that you're playing along to maintain discretion. Tell her later, in private, that while you may find such people agreeable to socialize with at times, their unenlightened, judgemental or ignorant attitude about women's sexuality is boring to you.

More simply put: just keeping your mouth shut will go a lot further than most men.

Reducing ASD in LTRs

Men in long-term relationships wanting to engage their women in deeper, more passionate sexuality need to start with themselves. In particular, as a man, you must ask yourself these questions:

- What really is acceptable and unacceptable female sexual behavior for me? (Dig deep, gentlemen.)
- How am I — as a man leading my relationship — prepared to take concrete action?

Most men have a vague notion of their feelings about the first point, and none at all about the second. In fact, most men aren't really aware they have any choice in the matter of the second point.

Once the above work has been started (it's a process; don't think you will ever finish it), taking a relationship to the next level generally follows one of two patterns:

1. The man attempts to logically persuade the woman.
2. The woman attempts to emotionally persuade the man.

You can see both patterns in nearly every issue of *Playboy's* "Advisor" column.

The first point never works. Not ever. The second is much more liable to work, except that not too many women are going to lead their relationship in a "sluttier" direction. More so today than ever before — to be sure — but this is still the exception rather than the rule. Not so surprisingly, for the second point, women tell of frustration in attempting to engage their men with activity beyond the men's comfort zones.

So, how to proceed?

The answer is simple!

Simply seduce your woman. That's all there is to it. Remember, it's impossible to seduce someone who is unwilling to be seduced. Let her be the "willing victim of circumstance;" let this be your gift to her.

Every time you desire a level of sexual engagement that is beyond either the social norm or her present comfort level, lead her there with confidence. Everything about seduction still applies in a long term relationship just as much as in a same night lay from a nightclub. You will have to build her attraction to you high enough to compel her to desire the risk. You must build comfort and rapport at this newer, deeper and riskier level of sexual engagement. You must be willing to handle ASD as it arises. And most importantly, you must be able to handle Last Minute Resistance from your woman exactly as if you just met her 3 hours before in a cafe. In a very real sense, you *are meeting a new woman*! Certainly, you are meeting an aspect of her personality that is previously unknown to you. She must always feel the emotional security that comes from being with a man who truly loves women.

19 Male Qualities Attractive to Women

A pretty man came to me
Never seen eyes so blue
I could not run away
It seemed we'd seen each other in a dream
It seemed like he knew me
— Magic Man, by Heart

NOW you know all about how the female mind works! In fact, you know things about feminine psychology that very, very few men will *ever* know. Experienced ladies men may know a lot of these things *subconsciously*, but never before has the true nuts and bolts of the female brain been laid out for you in such a way as we have done in this book.

Now, it's time to take a look at *ourselves* as men. It's one thing to understand what motivates women and what gets them sexually aroused. It's quite another matter to actually *be* a man who is sexually appealing to women. So let's take a good, long look in the mirror and find where we can improve ourselves as men who love women deeply.

Looks

Do you think that women care a lot about a man's looks? Before we answer that question, here's another: have you ever seen a woman being drawn to a particular man and found yourself scratching your head in amazement? You look at the guy, and you think to yourself, "That guy is as ugly as home-made sin, what in the world does she *see* in him?."[1] While many good looking men have beautiful women in their lives, many do not.

Good looks can, in fact, *hinder* your success with women. A

[1]Joseph: I recall many such experiences while growing up. I would say to myself, "it can't be his looks, he's very ugly! At least by the standards I've seen on television. What is going on here?" It took me years to understand what was *really* going on.

very good looking, handsome, or dapper man is *expected* to be an expert with women. Such a man lacking expert qualities suffers under the label of "creepy." This is due to a phenomenon called *congruence*. A man who looks like he is good with women *should* be good with women. This is a situation that worsens with age. Really good-looking, younger guys can get away with quite a bit, especially with older women who find such naive incongruence to be cute or charming. Furthermore, without very careful calibration, women who cannot match you in looks may well refuse your advances, feeling that all a good-looking guy would want with her is easy sex. Thus, whether you look like a male model or not, you need *game* to consistently get what you want!

What one woman finds attractive is often another woman's definition of dog food. It's that subjective. We have also discov-ered that when it comes to looks, men put priority on different facets than women do. Of course, women prefer tall men with muscular bodies, right? However, if a man possesses certain *other* attributes besides just good looks, what we will call Al-pha Attributes, he will actually be rated as better looking by the women in the study. Conversely men who appear [2] good look-ing in photographs, will later be ranked several points lower on the looks scale if they are deficient in the Alpha Attributes.

Alpha Atributes

Before we discuss some of the Alpha Attributes that you will want to cultivate in yourself, let's posit for now that good looks are a somewhat of a help in your success with women. If you are naturally good looking, you might have a certain advantage at the outset, and we won't deny that. However, as you will soon discover, there are other qualities that you must have which are far more important.

In Chapter 4 (Female Basic Conflict), we examined in detail how, instinctually, women have two primary needs when it

[2] Women will tell you these men "look good on paper."

comes to selecting a mate. First, they need a man with fierce, strong genes to mate with. This is where sexual attraction comes into play. Women also need emotional and financial support during times of pregnancy and childbirth and through the infancy of the child. True, modern society has conferred many benefits onto women such that they usually no longer need a specific man to fulfill the role of "provider." Whether consciously or unconsciously, however, women will typically view a man as either a potential Lover, or a potential Provider, or some combination of these two types. It is crucial to understand this distinction, which all women make with the men in their lives.

What then, about material wealth? Well, whether you are a Lover or a Provider, having wealth will certainly help you with your goals in life. But again, like good looks, it is not even a primary criteria for attracting a woman sexually. (Recall from Chapter 7 — Female Archetypes — that a Materialista is a woman who is not motivated by sexual attraction but by money or material possessions).

It is true that we are constantly bombarded with media images telling us that a man on one knee who has just spent three month's worth of his salary to buy a stone for a woman is what makes him sexually attractive. And we know that both men and women love to receive gifts. But demonstrating that you put your woman on a pedestal, or displaying your capability as a potential Provider, is not at all the same thing as cooking up sexual attraction within a woman. As you will soon discover, sexual attraction does not get sparked within a woman based on the size of your bank account or even by your genuine displays of love towards her.

A man's ability to generate and grow wealth does in fact signal the presence of other, more important qualities within the man, such as leadership, intelligence, survivability and so forth.

What is an "Alpha" male? According to dictionary.com, Alpha Male simply refers to a man who is the dominant member within a group of males. Women are irresistibly drawn to the Alpha Male. It's instinctual: a woman cannot help but feel deep sexual attraction when she is in the presence of an Alpha Male. Her instincts signal to her that he is a leader of men, he is a survivor. He is so strong that competition from other males — which is a reality in life — does not phase him at all, in fact, he thrives on it. Her evolutionary instincts signal unmistakably that this is a man she would like to mate with. In plain English, we say "he makes her horny."

Naturally, then, we will want to cultivate the traits of an Alpha Male. More than just putting on an act, we must *become* the Alpha Male. We've already explained in great detail how a woman will test you to see whether you are putting on an act or if you are the real deal. To become an Alpha Male can sometimes take years of practice and study, but great improvements can be made starting today, as soon as you set this book down on your coffee table. What, then, are some of the key characteristics of the Alpha Male?

Impudence is the most tell-tale trait of the Alpha Male: that ability to raise a finger, saluting the absurdity of life, and face the consequences with a smile or smirk. Another way in which we demonstrate impudence is by displaying our ability to take a woman sexually. Everyone knows that heterosexual men like to have sex with beautiful women, but due to society's constraints and that mental illness that we've referred to earlier as the Madonna/whore Complex, men hold back.[3] Such men act overly polite and gentlemanly, so as not to offend the woman's supposed delicate sensibilities. The *impudent* man, on the other hand, *takes what he wants*. An impudent man is not intimidated by beauty and is not afraid to create the circumstances to entice a beautiful woman into willing submission.

Sexual Confidence Another reason why being a sexually confident male is attractive to women is because it demonstrates that you have *sexual competence*. Women don't want to just have sex; they can get plain old sex anywhere and any time. What women *do* want, what women intensely crave, is *great* sex. We are confident about the things we know we are good at. Therefore, when we display sexual confidence, we are send-

[3]"Taking" a beautiful woman is not an endorsement for forced sex any more than capitalism is an endorsement for bank robbery.

ing a powerful message to the woman: we know what we are doing and we know how to blow her mind! That's instantly attractive to a woman.

Voice Quality. We defer to popular authority on this one: "US researchers got 149 men and women to rate the attractiveness of a series of recorded voices. They found the most appealing voices belonged to people who had sex at an earlier age, had more sexual partners and were more prone to infidelity." [4] We refuse to speculate whether voice quality is cause or effect!

Leader of Men, Protector of Women. When you demonstrate that you understand the potential danger a woman faces if she acts out sexually, and that you are a man that can shield her from those consequences, then you are naturally going to be attractive to her. Most women are not impressed by a man who finds himself in bar fights or other unnecessary physical altercations. But she will want to know she is safe with you and that you're not afraid to act in cases where it's absolutely necessary. It's really important to recognize that rushing to a woman's defense is *rarely* necessary. A man who doesn't understand this subtle point is going to create the opposite effect in women to what he intends.

Mission and Honor. Take away from a man his mission and his honor, take away from him the feeling that he is useful to his women and his children, and you kill him emotionally. Men understand instinctively that without respect, there is no chance for love. As a man, you'll want to be steadfast in your mission in life, whatever you might choose for that to be. And you'll want to be sure that your principles and your mission in life is without compromise, *especially* in cases where a woman might try to divert you from them. A woman really doesn't want a man to give up his mission or compromise his honor for her, but she *is* interested to know if a man will easily be led to do so.

Decisiveness has many aspects, the most notable of which is the ability to make an appropriate decision when under mental, emotional or physical stress. This could be called "Decisive

[4] http://news.bbc.co.uk/2/hi/health/3665246.stm

Leadership" and has a very important place in relationships.

Dominance and Social Status

Male Sexual Dominance is a complex of behavioral responses from a man meant to lead the woman and her emotions into sex. Male Sexual Dominance is actually an important precondition for a woman to become sexually aroused. The "Cocky and Funny" attitude, popularized by David DeAngelo, is a pattern of behavior that constitutes sexual dominance over the female, without the need for *physical* dominance. This style of behavior does indeed elicit sexual arousal in females. By withdrawing rapport from the female, and by displaying a cocky but funny or playful attitude, the male is behaving in a sexually dominant way and is thereby able to arouse the female sexually.

Just as visual stimulus is a great factor in increasing a man's sexual desire, a man's *social status* has a tremendous impact on *female* sexual desire. This means that a certain characteristic in the male elicits a certain neurobiological response in the recipient.

Of course, the fact that women will respond preferentially to men displaying the traits indicative of high mate value does not imply that women *consciously* appraise men through the sharp eye of material pragmatism in every case.

When a woman experiences feelings of sexual attraction, she is not, at a conscious level, plotting a reproductive strategy designed to maximize the representation of her genes in future generations. Rather, she is probably simply experiencing sexual desire for the man in question. This desire may or may not enhance her reproductive success in the milieu where it is experienced.

Practical Advice

When you start to apply the counsel in this book and adopt the traits of the alpha male, you will find that competition among women for your time and company can in fact become quite fierce. As men who have made such a transformation, we can tell you first hand that you will experience astonishment at the reactions you begin to receive from women, along with a deep sense of satisfaction.

Warning! women *will* test you, and *test you hard*. As we have discussed, females have a biological imperative to select only the best males to have sexual relationships with. Therefore, quite simply, women will test you in order to determine whether you truly possess those Alpha traits or are just a fake, only *pretending* to be an Alpha Male. A woman becomes consciously aware that she is in the presence of an attractive male, but at the same time her instincts drive her to make certain choices. Therefore, these tests will be both conscious and subconscious from the woman's perspective.

The important thing is to recognize these tests when they come, and to not take them personally in a negative way. The testing is "personal," in the sense that they are directed at you, but the good news is that it generally means that the woman likes you and has at least some attraction for you. Why? Because if she were not attracted to you, she wouldn't bother spending any time with you at all!

Men that are orbiters will generally say that their relationships with these women are generally good and that they cannot understand why she is not attracted sexually when they "do everything for her." What such a man has missed is that the woman has already tested him and found him lacking as a sexual being. He is now in the role of male girlfriend, or benefactor, and as long as he maintains that role, she has no reason to argue with him or test him as a sexual male. She will, of course, still test him from time to time to ensure that the dinners, drinks and emotional comfort are always available to her.

Since testing is so closely related to the mechanisms controlling sexual attraction, it is important to remember that *testing never ends*. Maintaining an appropriate level of attraction within the relationship is important. Some of the ways in which the authors of this book maintain attraction with our mates are:

- Regular, *social* interaction with men who are attractive to women. Uncalibrated and unattractive men induce the risk of socially awkward situations and won't help you to mature into a more attractive man.
- Clear demonstration of physical leadership in our daily lives. We are each living our lives in a manner congruent with our beliefs, with gusto and without apology.
- Regular, *social* interaction with other attractive females. Women are social creatures, and will derive emotional satisfaction from being with a man capable of being with a variety of women.

Normal, social interactions with attractive women are critical for several reasons. Within the hothouse of a relationship, interactions between men and women can assume bizarre and ultimately unhealthy forms without socially calibrating expe-riences with normal, healthy women outside the relationship. Direct, personal feedback from women allows us to calibrate our behavior *within* the relationship. When we are passing tests thrown by women *outside* the relationship, we have a baseline for our own behavior *inside* the relationship. For those of you who enjoy jealous women (we do not), this could inspire a cer-tain amount of jealousy, which also increases attraction, so calibrate accordingly.

Men, note well: encourage your woman to maintain normal, regular social interaction with males of her acquaintance. If you are the man of her dreams, her Prince, you have nothing to fear.

Bibliography

[1] Matt Ridley. *The Red Queen: Sex and the Evolution of Human Nature.*

[2] Robin Baker. *Sperm Wars.* Thunder's Mouth Press, 245 W. 17th St., New York, NY 10011, 2006. Infidelity, Sexual Conflict, and Other Bedroom Battles.

[3] Geoffrey F. Miller. *The Mating Mind: How Sexual Choice Shaped the Evolution of Human Nature.* Anchor Books, Random House, New York, NY, 2000.

[4] Leil Lowndes. *Undercover Sex Signals.* Kensington Publishing Corp., 850 Third Avenue, New York, NY 10022, 2001. A Pickup Guide for Guys.

[5] Tracey Cox. *SuperFlirt.* DK Publishing, Inc, 375 Hudson Street, New York NY 10014, 2003.

[6] John Gray. *Men are from Mars, Women are from Venus.* Harper Collins, 1993.

[7] Louanne Brizendine. *The Female Brain.* Morgan Road/Random House, 2006, 2006.

[8] Robert Greene. *The Art of Seduction.* Joost Elffers, 2004.

[9] Ron Louis and David Copeland. *How to Succeed with Women.* Prentice Hall Press, 1998.

[10] Meredith L. Chivers, Gerulf Rieger, Elizabeth Latty, and J. Michael Bailey. A sex difference in the specificity of sexual arousal. *Psychological Science*, 15(11):736–744, 2004.

[11] Robert A. Glover. *No More Mr Nice Guy.* Running Press Book Publishers, 125 South Twenty-second Street, Philadelphia PA 19103, 2003. A Proven Plan for Getting What You Want in Love, Sex and Life.

[12] Eric Berne. *Games People Play: the Psychology of Human Relations.* Ballantine, New York, 1964.

[13] David Deida. *The Way of the Superior Man*. Sounds True, Inc., Boulder,CO 80306, 2004. A Spiritual Guide to Mastering the Challenges of Women, Work, and Sexual Desire.

[14] Ellen Fein and Sherrie Scheider. *The Rules*. Grand Central Publishing, 2007.

[15] Leil Lowndes. *How to Make Anyone Fall In Love With You*. Contemporary Books, 4255 West Touhy Avenue, Lincolnwood, IL 60712, 1995.

[16] Robert B. Cialdini. *Influence*. Allyn and Bacon, 160 Gould Street, Needham Heights, MA 02494, 2001. Science and Practice.

[17] Carryl P. Navalta, Ann Polcari, Danielle M. Webster, Ani Boghassian, and Martin H. Teicher. Effects of childhood sexual abuse on neuropsychological and cognitive function in college women. *J Neuropsychiatry Clin Neurosci*, 18:45–53, February 2006.

[18] G. Sanders and L. Roos-Field. Neuropsychological development of cognitive abilities: a new research strategy and some preliminary evidence for a sexual orientation model. *Int J Neurosci*, 36(1-2):1–16, September 1987. Basing on this study childhood sexual abuse causes cognitive impairment (LSE theory).

[19] A. P. Arnold. Sex chromosomes and brain gender. *Nat Rev Neurosci*, 5(9):701–709, 2004. Prenatal sexual hormones influence sexual orientation, homosexual males resemble heterosexual women more than heterosexual females.

[20] W. Wood and A. H. Eagly. A cross-cultural analysis of the behavior of women and men: Implications for the origins of sex difference. *Psychological Bulletin*, 128:699–727, 2002. Sex chromosomes probably determine the gender (sexually dimorphic phenotype) of the brain. Male and female brains are genetically different.

[21] C. Bostic St. Clair and J. Grinder. *Whispering In The Wind*. J & C Enterprises, Scotts Valley, California 95066, 2001.

[22] A. Aleman and M. Wout. Subvocalization in auditory-verbal imagery: just a form of motor imagery? *Cognitive Processing*, 5(4):228–231, 2004.

[23] L. Fadiga dn L. Fogasi, G. Pavesi, and G Rizzolatti. Motor facilitation during action observation: a magnetic simulation study. *Journal of Neurophysiology*, 73:2608–2611, 1995.

[24] A. N. Meltzoof and W. Prinz. *The Imitative Mind*, chapter The Imitative mind: Development, Evolution and Brain Bases, pages 19–41. Cambridge University Press, Cambridge, 2002.

[25] A. N. Meltzoff and M. K. Moore. Imitation of facial and manual gestures by human neonates. *Science*, 198:75–78, 1977.

[26] M. Iacoboni. *Perspectives on imitation: from cognitive neuroscience to social science*, chapter Understanding others: imitation, language, empathy. MIT Press, Cambridge, MA, 2007.

[27] V. Gallese, L. Fadiga, L. Fogassia, and G. Rizzolatti. Action recognition in the premotor cortex. *Brain*, 119:593–609, 1996.

[28] D. A. Overton. State-dependent or dissociated learning produced with pentobarbital. *J Comp Physiol Psychol*, pages 3–12, 1964.

[29] V. S. Ramachandran. Mirror neurons and imitation learning as the driving force behind the great leap forward in human evolution. *Edge*, 2000.

[30] G. Rizzolatti and L. Craighero. The mirror-neuron system. *Annual Review of Neuroscience*, 27:169–192, 2004.

[31] G. Rizzolatti, L. Fogassi, and V. Gallese. Neurophysiological mechanisms underlying the understanding and imitation of action. *Nature Reviews Neuroscience*, pages 661–669, 2001.

[32] K. Stefan, L. G. Cohen, J. Duque, R. Mazzochio, P. Celnik, and L. Sawaki. Formation of a motor memory by action observation. *The Journal of Neuroscience*, 25(41):9339–9346, 2005.

[33] Autumn Stephens. *The Secret Lives of Lawfully Wedded Wives*. Inner Ocean Publishing, P. O. Box 1239, Makawao, Maui, HI 96768, 2006. *27 Women Writers on Love, Infidelity, Sex Roles, Race, Kids, and More*.

[34] Jan L. Shifren, Glenn D. Braunstein, James A. Simon, Peter R. Casson, John E. Buster, Geoffrey P. Raymond, Regula E. Burki, Elizabeth S. Ginsburg, Raymond C. Rosen, Sandra R. Leiblum, Kim E. Caramelli, Norman A. Mazer, Kirtley P. Jones, and Claire A. Daugherty. Transdermal testosterone treatment in women with impaired sexual function after oophorectomy. *N Engl J Med.*, 343(10):682–688, 2000.

[35] Anatoly Protopopov. The treatise of love, as it is recognized by awful bore. http://www.geocities.com/protopop_1999/treatise.html (second edition, 1999.

[36] Theresa L. Crenshaw. *The Alchemy of Love and Lust*. Putnam Pub Group, 1996.

[37] James Allen. *As a Man Thinketh*. DeVorss & Company, P.O. Box 1389, Camarillo CA 93011-1389, 1902.

[38] Tariq "K-Flex" Nasheed. *The Art of Mackin*. Research Associates School Times Publications, 751 East 75th Street, Chicago, IL 60619, 2000.

[39] Michael J. Bader. *Arousal : the secret logic of sexual fantasies*. Thomas Dunne Books, St. Martin's Press, 175 Fifth Avenue, New York, NY 10010, 2002.

[40] Mickey Royal. *The Pimp Game : an instructional manual*. Mikail Sharif, 1998.

[41] Neil Strauss. *The Game : penetrating the secret society of pickup artists*. HarperCollins, 10 East 53rd Street, New York, NY 10022, 2005.

[42] Leil Lowndes. *How to be a people magnet : finding friends and lovers and keeping them for life*. McGraw-Hill, Two Penn Plaza, New York, NY 10121-2298, 2001.

[43] Terry Gould. *The Lifestyle*. Random House Canada, 1999.

[44] Jack Morin. *The Erotic Mind*. HarperCollins, 10 East 53rd Street, New York, NY 10022, 1995.

[45] Paradise. *21st Century Fox, Space Age Pimping*. Infinite Dreams, P.O. Box 63, Buxton, SK17 9XH, Great Britain, 2001.

[46] Erving Goffman. *Interaction Ritual*. Doubleday & Company, Inc., 1967.

[47] Julius Fast. *Social Intelligence*. Simon & Schuster, Inc., 1230 Avenue of the Americas, New York, NY 10020, 1970.

[48] Jayne Ann Krentz. *Dangerous men & adventurous women : romance writers on the appeal of the romance*. University of Pennsylvania Press, Philadelphia, PA 19104-6005, 1992.

[49] Brian Tracy and Ron Arden. *The Power of Charm*. Amacom, American Management Association, 1601 Broadway, New York, NY 10019, 2006.

[50] Daniel Goleman. *Social Intelligence*. Bantam Dell, Random House, New York, NY, 2006.

A Glossary of Terms

Subcommunication: The underlying or implied meaning behind direct communication. Women's favored method of communication with each other and with members of the opposite sex.

Betaization: The process by which a man loses his leadership position to the female in the relationship. This can happen suddenly or imperceptibly over time. Women are unconsciously driven towards this process; they will inexorably lose sexual attraction for the man who allows this process to continue unabated.

LTR: A long-term relationship with an expectation of monogamy between the man and the woman.

MLTR: Multiple long-term relationships. Similar to LTR, except without monogamy; there is the possibility or reality of other, simultaneous relationships for either the man or the woman or both of them.

EFA: The Early Frame Announcement. A woman's subcommunicated declaration, very early on in the relationship, of her inflexible terms for the relationship.

Female Logic: Women have a unique method of communicating emotions that is often baffling to men. Neurological studies and especially our own field experience have demonstrated that men and women use different parts of the brain to reach conclusions on important matters, and that our primary goals when it comes to dating and mating can often be in conflict.

Magic Pussy Syndrome (MPS): The belief that because a woman possesses a pussy, she is entitled to special privileges at other people's expense. This is an endemic cultural phenomenon in modern, western society.

Good Girl: A woman whose primary motivation when it comes to relationships with men is the relationship itself.

Adventuress: A woman who is primarily concerned with male attention and validation, and her own selfish pleasure.

Materialista: A woman who is primarily concerned with the material benefits she can derive from her relationships with men.

HD: High Sex Drive. A woman with a higher-than-average sex drive.

LD: Low Sex Drive. A woman with a lower-than-average sex drive.

HSE: High Self Esteem. A woman with a high level of Basic Trust.

LSE: Low Self Esteem. A woman with a low level of Basic Trust.

Basic Trust: An degree of inner sureness that a person has that their inner and external worlds will be safe and happy places for them, as opposed to places of turmoil and unmanageable conflict.

AB Indecision: The presentation of two or more choices — both equally agreeable to the man — which are then disqualified by the woman on emotional rather than logical grounds.

Printed in Great Britain
by Amazon

65872f6f-7c9f-40af-bc61-9c03a088f016R01